Win at Bridge
with
Jacoby & Son

Win at Bridge
with
Jacoby & Son

By

OSWALD and JAMES JACOBY

G. P. Putnam's Sons   New York

Preface

IT is not inhospitable to trim your guests when they drop in for a few rubbers of bridge. You should play your best if you expect them to come back for more punishment. And this book is dedicated to making you a winning player.

Bridge is a friendly game, even when you lose. It teaches you to think, to use your imagination and to avoid doing certain things again. It also teaches you how to recognize facts, including the one that you can't win 'em all but you can make your opponents feel as if they have been through a battle.

There are certain standards of bidding and concepts of play that are recognized as "success-prone." They are not infallible, and they are not even rigid. When we say you should have 26 points in the North-South hands for a major suit or no-trump game, we are not saying that you can't make a game with 24, or that you can't go set with 28. When we say that minor-suit overcalls are more harmful than good, we do not mean you should never make one.

You learn by experience that there are exceptions to rules and you learn how to recognize the exceptions. Hands in this book are drawn from all types of players — experts, average players, even bad players. They have been chosen to illustrate how to get the most out of the cards you are dealt, and sometimes even a little more than the cards deserve.

We must assume that those who read this book are at least average players, who know the fundamentals of contract bridge, who play frequently and who want to improve their game. There should be many millions in this classification. But we have tried to make the text understandable to beginning students of the game, and there are millions more of them.

If you are a student, we have included an Appendix which lists the fundamentals of evaluating your high-card, distribution and supporting points. The rest of the book will be devoted to the bidding and playing of hands.

We will show how to find the methods that will offer chances of success, when several lines of play are offered. We will also try to show you how to understand what your partner and opponents mean when they play certain cards. And we will show you how to make your cards do their best.

If such terms as squeeze play, reverse play, elimination play, safety play and so on frighten you, remember that these are only names for things you may already be doing. They are far less complicated than they sound, and we believe that any player who can master the fundamentals of contract bridge can learn the advanced tactics.

In order to keep the book from being all study and no play, we will offer some unusual hands and examples of extraordinary skill. Some of them, as we have said, are hands played by average fans. Often these players bid and bring home contracts that an expert might misplay; occasionally they get themselves into ruinous contracts or blow a slam. Perhaps we can point out some of the pitfalls.

It is impossible for a player to get along without a system of bidding, one that will enable him and his partner to get to a reasonable contract. There are many systems, all based on similar standards. But unless there is an agreement as to what is needed to open the bidding and make the contract, all systems are in trouble.

We have placed an understandable stress on the Jacoby system, which we have tested in winning play. Fundamentally it is a standard system, differing in only a few details from many others.

For example, the Jacobys recommend from 15 to 17 high-card points and even distribution for an opening one no-trump bid. To respond with three no-trump, partner should have 11 high-card points or more. Some systems recommend 16 to 18 high-card points and balanced distribution, but require only 10 for a jump to game in no-trump. You will note that they all agree on the minimum safe requirement of 26 points for a no-trump game.

The Jacobys also endorse limit raises, the Jacoby transfer, the use of the Stayman convention and a few other things we will discuss. There may be a slight difference in the evaluation of the hand, but all systems are beginning to agree that distributional strength is as important as high-card points.

Keep in mind that bridge is a partnership game; it is of utmost importance that both members of the team use the same signals. Recommend this book to your regular partner and after you have picked up pointers, you will be surprised at how your bridge scores improve.

OSWALD and JAMES JACOBY

Contents

Win at Bridge
with
Jacoby & Son

1

The Opening Gun

ALL bridge games start with a biddable hand; if you hold one, it is a good policy to open the bidding if possible. An opening bid creates an advantage for your partnership.

An opening hand consists of *more than* 10 of the 40 high-card points in the deck. Your partnership should have *more than* 20 to compete successfully against your opponents.

Here are the *minimum* requirements for an opening suit bid of one:

  13 high-card points with 4-3-3-3 distribution.
  12 high-card points with any other distribution but no solid suit.
  11 high-card points with a six-card or good five-card suit.

Those are the high-card requirements. There are other considerations that make your hand stronger — or weaker — and these are to be taken into consideration if you go on with the bidding. Distribution values — short suits and voids — are very important, and points may be counted for these. After you have opened the bidding, your partner may count his distribution values; in addition he may add *supporting points* if he has better than average help in your suit. Frequently, a hand minimal in high-card values may be very strong in distribution.

Hand No. 1 was played in the trials of the International

Championship match in 1965. Almost any average pair would have no trouble reaching game in spades with this hand.

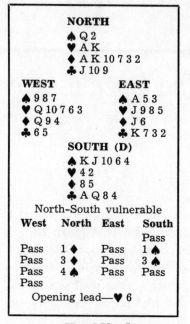

NORTH
♠ Q 2
♥ A K
♦ A K 10 7 3 2
♣ J 10 9

WEST
♠ 9 8 7
♥ Q 10 7 6 3
♦ Q 9 4
♣ 6 5

EAST
♠ A 5 3
♥ J 9 8 5
♦ J 6
♣ K 7 3 2

SOUTH (D)
♠ K J 10 6 4
♥ 4 2
♦ 8 5
♣ A Q 8 4

North–South vulnerable

West	North	East	South
			Pass
Pass	1 ♦	Pass	1 ♠
Pass	3 ♦	Pass	3 ♠
Pass	4 ♠	Pass	Pass
Pass			

Opening lead—♥ 6

Hand No. 1

The bidding shown was normal. South has only 10 high-card points and a five-card spade suit. He does not have *more than* 10, and the only distribution points he can count are two doubletons. He is in no position to open.

However, his partner, North, has 17 high-card points, plus a six-card diamond suit. He must open and bids a diamond. Now South can bid, for the hand that had only ten points is a very good supporting hand, even though it contains only two small diamonds. He bids his spades.

North shows his power by jumping to three diamonds. South bids three spades, and North, knowing that South has at least a five-card spade suit because South rebid, can now boost the contract to four.

There is no problem in the play. South must lose the ace of

trumps, but even though his opponents opened with hearts and led another heart after taking the ace of spades, he can finesse the king of clubs and make six without the necessity of setting up diamonds.

In the Championship trials, however, under the stress of keen competition, two Souths opened the bidding with one spade, thus starting the attack without enough ammunition. Fortunately these two Souths found their partners strong, but the partners forced the bidding to six. The club finesse worked just as well on a slam contract as it did on a game contract and instead of being punished for a bad bid, the two Souths were rewarded, even though there was no play for slam without a successful club finesse.

It is often said that one cannot argue with success. However, do not make bids like South's opening spade a way of life, because you will be punished more often than rewarded.

Hand No. 2 illustrates this point.

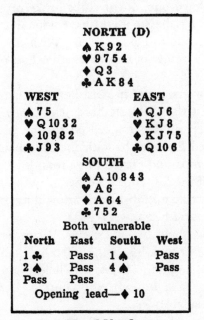

NORTH (D)
♠ K 9 2
♥ 9 7 5 4
♦ Q 3
♣ A K 8 4

WEST
♠ 7 5
♥ Q 10 3 2
♦ 10 9 8 2
♣ J 9 3

EAST
♠ Q J 6
♥ K J 8
♦ K J 7 5
♣ Q 10 6

SOUTH
♠ A 10 8 4 3
♥ A 6
♦ A 6 4
♣ 7 5 2

Both vulnerable

North	East	South	West
1 ♣	Pass	1 ♠	Pass
2 ♠	Pass	4 ♠	Pass
Pass	Pass		

Opening lead—♦ 10

Hand No. 2

North, the dealer, has but 12 high-card points. He might have added a thirteenth point for his doubleton queen-three of diamonds, but he had a fairly balanced hand otherwise. He opened one club.

South, his partner, had a very good supporting hand, three aces, a total of 12 high-card points and a five-card spade suit, plus an ace doubleton in hearts. He was entitled, with the five-card suit, to figure his hand at 13 points. Assuming that North had opened with the equivalent of 13, there was a game in sight. (A count of 26 is usually enough for a major suit or no-trump game.)

He bid spades, North showed support, which in this case he had, and South, assuming that there were 26 points in the hand, went to four spades.

South played the queen of diamonds from dummy on West's opening lead of a ten. East's king was captured by South's ace. South realized that he would probably lose a trick in each suit and wind up down one, but if clubs broke properly and if the defense slipped a trifle, he might have hope. He led his seven of clubs and let it ride to East's queen. (With the ace and king of clubs in dummy it did not matter whether East played the queen or the ten.)

Most East players would have cashed the diamond jack immediately, but East was thinking hard at that point. His diamond trick would keep and he attacked hearts immediately.

South covered East's eight with the ace, then cashed the ace and king of trumps, and played three rounds of clubs. He hoped East would ruff the last club with his queen of spades, but East kept out of the trap and discarded a low diamond, while South got rid of his losing heart.

But South still held two diamonds. When he led a diamond from dummy, East took his jack, cashed his high trump and led his remaining diamond to West, who held the nine.

South might have brought the contract home if East had trumped the final club lead.

You can see that bidding and the interpretation of your partner's bids, as well as the bids of your opponents, have a great deal of weight in reaching the right contract. Bidding is far from being an exact science, and experts vary considerably.

In the International team trials in 1965, there were nine tables of experts at work. One might expect that the bidding of many hands would be identical, but this was not the case. Not until deal eight of round four did any hand produce nearly the same results.

Hand No. 3 is one of the later hands; the bidding was standard. It is interesting for the fact that an expert managed to go down, while an average player would have made his contract.

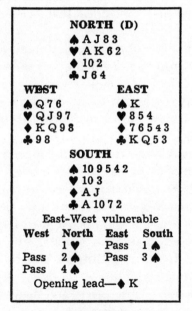

NORTH (D)
♠ A J 8 3
♥ A K 6 2
♦ 10 2
♣ J 6 4

WEST
♠ Q 7 6
♥ Q J 9 7
♦ K Q 9 8
♣ 9 8

EAST
♠ K
♥ 8 5 4
♦ 7 6 5 4 3
♣ K Q 5 3

SOUTH
♠ 10 9 5 4 2
♥ 10 3
♦ A J
♣ A 10 7 2

East-West vulnerable

West	North	East	South
	1 ♥	Pass	1 ♠
Pass	2 ♠	Pass	3 ♠
Pass	4 ♠		

Opening lead—♦ K

Hand No. 3

North, the dealer, had a minimum opening and he bid a heart; his partner, with two aces and some extra values, bid one spade. North raised to two spades and South rebid his five-card suit and wound up in a four-spade contract. Practically every South player in the trials reached this contract although the·play for it is less than a 50 percent chance. But in this type of tournament play the scoring encourages the bidding of doubtful game contracts.

The ordinary player would make the contract because the king and queen of clubs are in the East hand.

But one expert won the king of diamonds lead with the ace and led a spade to finesse dummy's eight. East took the trick with his singleton king and returned the three of diamonds. West won with the queen and led the queen of hearts. South played the ace from dummy and played the king of hearts, then returned to his hand by ruffing the third heart. Then he led a spade and finessed dummy's jack. East showed out and South counted the hand and concluded that West probably started with two clubs.

South played the jack of clubs from dummy and East covered with the king. South won with the ace as West dropped the eight.

Now South led another trump to dummy's ace and played a second club. East played low and South had to decide whether West's remaining club was the queen or the nine. He made the wrong decision and West won with the nine. South still had to lose to the queen of clubs and was down one.

An average player would have played the ten of clubs.

Some experts never open a four-card suit. Others never open a four-card spade suit, but will open a heart four-carder. Others tend not to open any major suit of four cards and others do so with reasonable frequency. But no expert opens four-card majors indiscriminately. Thus, even those who say they open four-card majors don't do so often, and many who say they do not will open one heart with a hand such as South holds in Hand No. 4.

South's hearts are strong and in all probability he can handle three-card trump support. If he opens one diamond, it will be difficult for him to get to a heart bid later, so he opens a heart and looks to his diamonds as a convenient rebid. The key play

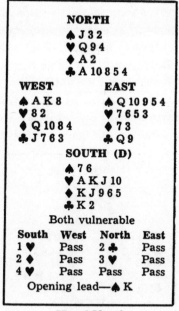

NORTH
♠ J 3 2
♥ Q 9 4
♦ A 2
♣ A 10 8 5 4

WEST
♠ A K 8
♥ 8 2
♦ Q 10 8 4
♣ J 7 6 3

EAST
♠ Q 10 9 5 4
♥ 7 6 5 3
♦ 7 3
♣ Q 9

SOUTH (D)
♠ 7 6
♥ A K J 10
♦ K J 9 6 5
♣ K 2

Both vulnerable

South	West	North	East
1 ♥	Pass	2 ♣	Pass
2 ♦	Pass	3 ♥	Pass
4 ♥	Pass	Pass	Pass

Opening lead—♠ K

Hand No. 4

at four hearts is that South must not lead trumps, but make the hand by a cross-ruff.

The defense starts with three spade leads and South ruffs the third, then cashes his ace and king of diamonds and his club ace and king. This gives him five tricks; five trumps on cross-ruffs make the ten needed for the heart game.

If you avoid bidding four-card majors, it is often necessary to bid a three-card minor. Many people today play what is generally called "the forcing club" or "short club." This so-called convention has almost as many interpretations as the number of people who play it. It means in general that an opening club shows good high-card count but no biddable suit and that the partner must show a four-card major, if he has one.

Every expert bids three-card club suits on occasion, but not one bids the "short" club. When an expert opens one club it is not a forcing bid; his partner knows that he has at least three clubs to an honor.

A corporal's guard of experts uses a formalized one-club convention which guarantees a certain minimum high-card strength and shows nothing about clubs at all. This is the "big club" and has no relation to the "short club." The big club is a legitimate bid, although it has very few followers.

Hand No. 5 shows North opening with a three-card club suit. North hopes his partner will respond in a major, but even with 20 points, he does not expect to make game if his partner passes.

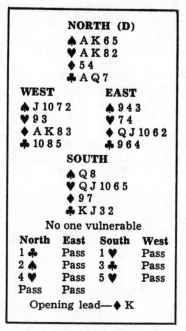

NORTH (D)
♠ A K 6 5
♥ A K 8 2
♦ 5 4
♣ A Q 7

WEST
♠ J 10 7 2
♥ 9 3
♦ A K 8 3
♣ 10 8 5

EAST
♠ 9 4 3
♥ 7 4
♦ Q J 10 6 2
♣ 9 6 4

SOUTH
♠ Q 8
♥ Q J 10 6 5
♦ 9 7
♣ K J 3 2

No one vulnerable

North	East	South	West
1 ♣	Pass	1 ♥	Pass
2 ♠	Pass	3 ♣	Pass
4 ♥	Pass	5 ♥	Pass
Pass	Pass		

Opening lead—♦ K

Hand No. 5

South, with 9 high-card points, shows his five-card heart suit, in preference to a raise in clubs. North jumps to two spades, showing his strength. South shows his club support. North bids four hearts. South reappraises his hand and thinks it is worth a slam try. But he is worried about the unbid suit, diamonds. He bids five hearts and North, looking at two losing diamonds, passes. The hand is a laydown at five.

At this point, some irritated reader is going to shout: "The result was just the same as if a short club had been bid!" This is exactly the point. The short or forcing club is not necessary, and you might regret it. If your partner has nothing and you force him to bid, you are asking for trouble. You'll get to the two level and find that you have supported a four-card suit headed by a nine and have nowhere to go.

In 1935, the senior Jacoby's book, *The Four Aces System*, introduced a three-card minor-suit opening, for diamonds as well as clubs. It was a general utility bid, not intended to be psychic. The system was to be used only with a hand that had enough high-card points to make opening compulsory but had no satisfactory bid. The bid was also qualified by making it mandatory that the bidder have one of the three top honors in the suit he bid. Hand No. 6 shows such a bid.

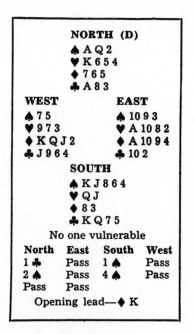

Hand No. 6

This three-card minor bid is now part of every system and in every expert's kit of bids. Furthermore, it has not changed one iota from the original concept. If the partner has a bad hand, he passes one club or one diamond, just as he would pass a heart or a spade opening.

In Hand No. 6, South responded one spade and when North supported, South went to game. The only problem is that the declarer has to go after hearts before he releases dummy's ace of clubs. Eventually South discards a club on dummy's king of hearts and he loses only two diamonds and the ace of hearts.

2

Howdy, Partner

AFTER partner opens the bidding, say with one heart, and the opponent to his left passes, it is your turn to bid. You do not know whether your partner has a weak hand or a strong one. But whether he opens four-card majors or not, you can assume he has some hearts. You should show your strength in your bidding: by raising, bidding a new suit or no-trump, jumping or passing.

To raise you should have four trumps in a minor or three in a major suit. To jump in the suit named by your partner you should have at least four trumps. For a single raise you need 7 to 10 points, including at least 3 high-card points. To make a double or jump raise, you should have 11 or 12 points, including at least 7 high-card points.

Triple raises require 13 or more points with at least 3 and not more than 10 high-card points. At this point, some deeply offended bridge player will scream: "I defy anyone to have a hand in which there are only 3 high-card points, but 13 points in all." Please refer to the Appendix, which gives fundamental instructions on how to appraise your hand. In responding, you count not only high-card and distribution points, but also supporting points, which includes all trumps over three. If you have a fistful of cards in your partner's suit, a triple raise shows exactly that kind of hand.

Jump raises should be nonforcing. Some players make it forcing to game, but many of them do not regard a jump in a minor suit forcing. If you want to make the jump forcing, you should revise your minimum count upward to 13-17 points, including 11 to 15 points in high cards.

To respond in a new suit at the one level you need 7 to 17 points, including at least 3 high-card points. (This, too, might involve a very long suit.) At the two level the requirement is 11 to 17 points, including at least 9 high-card points. In a jump shift, which means two of a higher suit or three of a lower suit than your partner bid, you need 18 points or more, including at least 11 high-card points.

The response of one no-trump can be made with 7 to 10 high-card points. This bid is made when you cannot raise your partner or bid a suit of your own at the one level.

Other no-trump responses show no-trump shape, including stoppers in all suits except the one your partner bid, and a definite number of high-card points: 13 or 14 for a jump to two no-trump, 15 to 17 to three no-trump.

There are occasional exceptions. Some hands cannot be bid by any rule, but you must remember that when you bid without values, your partner will believe you have them and trouble often results.

In Hand No. 7, two Los Angeles players, Ivan Erdos (South) and Kelsey Patterson, brought home a four-heart contract in the 1965 world championship tryouts. The bidding from one to four hearts is described as "papa-mama bidding."

South opened with 14 high-card points and an ace doubleton. North, with three trumps, made a minimum response, and East put in an intervening bid. South rebid hearts to three and when West raised his partner, North went to four hearts.

Ivan won the opening lead by putting his ace on West's queen of clubs. He decided he could not afford to lead trumps twice from dummy and played his heart king, which West ducked. Ivan ruffed a club in dummy and led a second heart from dummy. East played the jack and Ivan covered, knowing he

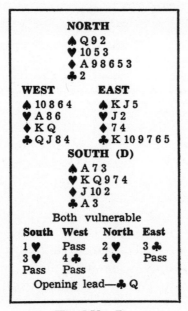

NORTH
♠ Q 9 2
♥ 10 5 3
♦ A 9 8 6 5 3
♣ 2

WEST
♠ 10 8 6 4
♥ A 8 6
♦ K Q
♣ Q J 8 4

EAST
♠ K J 5
♥ J 2
♦ 7 4
♣ K 10 9 7 6 5

SOUTH (D)
♠ A 7 3
♥ K Q 9 7 4
♦ J 10 2
♣ A 3

Both vulnerable

South	West	North	East
1 ♥	Pass	2 ♥	3 ♣
3 ♥	4 ♣	4 ♥	Pass
Pass	Pass		

Opening lead—♣ Q

Hand No. 7

would lose only one trump trick, which West took with his ace on this round.

Ivan would have made five, had West been kind enough to play a diamond or a club at this point, but West made his best possible return: the four of spades.

Ivan had to play the right spade from dummy, which was the deuce. East's jack forced Ivan's ace. Ivan then drew West's last trump and played the jack of diamonds to dummy's ace. A second diamond cleared the suit and Ivan unblocked by playing the ten from his hand. Had he not done this, he could not have returned to dummy to play the rest of his good diamonds.

West led the six of spades and once more Ivan had to decide which spade to play. He did not know whether East or West had the ten. East had made an overcall of three clubs and West had shown up with the queen of clubs, heart ace and king-queen of diamonds. It seemed likely that East's bid indicated a six-card club suit, in which case he would have short spades and West would hold the ten. Ivan played the nine and East's king of spades was the last trick for the defense.

Now we come to an old type of response that has recently been gaining favor, the limit raise. When you apply "limit" to any kind of a bridge bid, it means that this bid is restricted to a certain range of point count. For example, an opening one no-trump is a limit bid, because it shows from 15 to 17 or 16 to 18 points, depending on what system you play. You do not open one no-trump with more or less high-card points. The limit raise is in this category. Basically, the limit raise is a jump response to your partner's opening bid. It differs from the forcing jump raise in that it shows exactly 11 or 12 points, and is *not forcing*. If you use limit raises, of course, you will not use the jump as a force.

Practically all bridge books today talk about the raise of "two and one-half" when your hand has 11 or 12 points in support of your partner's opening bid. This means that if your partner opens with a suit, say a spade, and you have the count and trump support to encourage him, you do not raise him immediately. Instead you put in an intermediate bid of another suit, clubs or diamonds or the unbid major, and raise him the next time around.

Oswald Jacoby created this type of bidding when players shifted from limit bids to the forcing jump raises in the early thirties. Most European players stayed with the limit raise. The British Acol and the Swiss systems still use it. But without doubt, the limit raise is superior for showing strength. This is why the Jacoby system has decided to return to the old convention.

The opening one-spade bid in Hand No. 8 would be answered by a two-club call if you were using the "two and one-half" method. But the limit raise is used to advantage here. North had 10 high-card points, four trumps and a doubleton, which would figure 12 supporting points to a partner's opening. This is not enough to invite game with a force, but North can

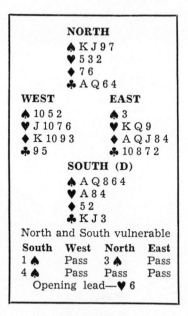

NORTH
♠ K J 9 7
♥ 5 3 2
♦ 7 6
♣ A Q 6 4

WEST
♠ 10 5 2
♥ J 10 7 6
♦ K 10 9 3
♣ 9 5

EAST
♠ 3
♥ K Q 9
♦ A Q J 8 4
♣ 10 8 7 2

SOUTH (D)
♠ A Q 8 6 4
♥ A 8 4
♦ 5 2
♣ K J 3

North and South vulnerable

South	West	North	East
1 ♠	Pass	3 ♠	Pass
4 ♠	Pass	Pass	Pass

Opening lead—♥ 6

Hand No. 8

make a limit raise of three spades. Because South has a trifle more than a minimum opening hand — 14 in high cards and a doubleton — he goes to game.

The hand is easily made after South wins the opening heart lead with his ace and draws trump. He discards one of his four losing red cards on dummy's fourth club and the contract is cold.

Had North responded two clubs, East might have put in a two-diamond bid and West might have given it a boost. Eventually, and this is pure speculation, East might wind up sacrificing at five diamonds. He would be down two tricks, but he would save game and rubber.

Hand No. 9 shows how to handle the forcing major suit raise in the Jacoby system.

North's hand would call for a three-spade response if the limit raise were not being played. North has 13 points in high cards, a doubleton and four trumps. Under the Jacoby limit-raise con-

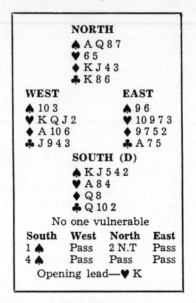

```
              NORTH
              ♠ A Q 8 7
              ♥ 6 5
              ♦ K J 4 3
              ♣ K 8 6
WEST                        EAST
♠ 10 3                      ♠ 9 6
♥ K Q J 2                   ♥ 10 9 7 3
♦ A 10 6                    ♦ 9 7 5 2
♣ J 9 4 3                   ♣ A 7 5
              SOUTH (D)
              ♠ K J 5 4 2
              ♥ A 8 4
              ♦ Q 8
              ♣ Q 10 2
         No one vulnerable
   South   West   North   East
   1 ♠     Pass   2 N.T   Pass
   4 ♠     Pass   Pass    Pass
      Opening lead—♥ K
```

Hand No. 9

vention, North bids two no-trump. This bid has nothing to do with no-trump, and your partner (and your opponents) must understand that this is the case when you use limit raises. It is a force and South must rebid and continue to rebid until a game contract is reached.

South goes immediately to four spades, showing a minimum hand and no interest in slam.

In minor suits, limit raises are even more logical than in majors. This is because a hand which will make nine tricks with normal luck will produce ten with a bit of good fortune. But there is still plenty of space between nine and eleven tricks.

South has no orthodox way to respond to his partner's diamond opening on Hand No. 10, except by making a limit raise to three diamonds. North looks his hand over and decides that five diamonds is out of the question, but perhaps three no-trump will work out.

North's first impulse is to bid three no-trump, but he spies

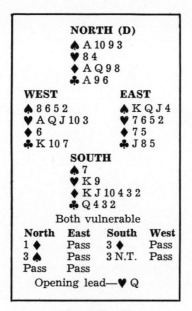

NORTH (D)
♠ A 10 9 3
♥ 8 4
♦ A Q 9 8
♣ A 9 6

WEST
♠ 8 6 5 2
♥ A Q J 10 3
♦ 6
♣ K 10 7

EAST
♠ K Q J 4
♥ 7 6 5 2
♦ 7 5
♣ J 8 5

SOUTH
♠ 7
♥ K 9
♦ K J 10 4 3 2
♣ Q 4 3 2

Both vulnerable

North	East	South	West
1 ♦	Pass	3 ♦	Pass
3 ♠	Pass	3 N.T.	Pass
Pass	Pass		

Opening lead—♥ Q

Hand No. 10

his worthless doubleton in hearts and decides that if three no-trump is to be played it would be far better to have South as declarer.

North bids three spades and South sees that he has potential stoppers in hearts and clubs and that his six diamonds probably would represent six tricks in no-trump. Since his partner's opening bid was in diamonds South bids three no-trump.

Should West open a spade, South will go down at least one trick, but West probably will lead a heart. This gives South his ninth trick — six in diamonds and the aces of clubs and spades.

Without limit raises, South would have to respond two clubs to his partner's opening diamond. West probably would bid two hearts and North and South undoubtedly would wind up playing some diamond contract. If they stop at three, they will show a profit, but if they get to five they will surely be set. At four, the result will depend on the kind of defense they have to contend with.

It will take you a little time to get used to playing limit raises. The most difficult adjustment will be to train yourself to use the unusual no-trump bid. It will require practice to avoid bidding two no-trump when you have a natural two-no-trump response. But once you grow accustomed to it, you will find that you have improved your bidding considerably. It has been our experience that the two no-trump response to show 13 to 15 high-card points with stoppers in all unbid suits and a no-trump pattern is just about as useless a bid as there is.

In the Jacoby limit raises, the two no-trump response by an unpassed hand to a major suit opening is designed to show strength. But if you have a no-trump hand, how do you get to a no-trump contract?

In Hand No. 11, North opens with one spade. South has stoppers in hearts, diamonds and clubs and has no-trump distribution; he feels that a no-trump contract would be more profitable than spades. Therefore, under the Jacoby system he responds two clubs and after North's spade rebid, South jumps to three no-trump.

In this hand there is a problem in making the contract. South holds off twice on the diamond leads, but he must win the third diamond. He runs off four club tricks and each opponent discards a heart. Next he leads a low spade to dummy. West plays low and South puts in dummy's nine. East wins and leads a heart.

The way the cards lie, South will make the rest of the tricks because the heart finesse will work and the spades will break. But South does not know this and must make a decision.

He knows that if he finesses he will risk a two-trick set and the finesse is a 50-50 proposition. But West showed five diamonds to his partner's two and each defender had produced three clubs. Therefore the odds are that East will hold the king of hearts. He finesses and wins.

A limit raise can often make the path to a slam a little easier. In Hand No. 12, North shows a hand with good trumps and 11

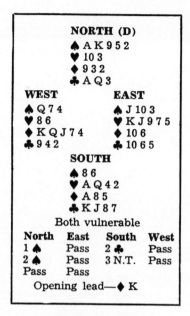

NORTH (D)
♠ A K 9 5 2
♥ 10 3
♦ 9 3 2
♣ A Q 3

WEST
♠ Q 7 4
♥ 8 6
♦ K Q J 7 4
♣ 9 4 2

EAST
♠ J 10 3
♥ K J 9 7 5
♦ 10 6
♣ 10 6 5

SOUTH
♠ 8 6
♥ A Q 4 2
♦ A 8 5
♣ K J 8 7

Both vulnerable

North	East	South	West
1 ♠	Pass	2 ♣	Pass
2 ♠	Pass	3 N.T.	Pass
Pass	Pass		

Opening lead—♦ K

Hand No. 11

or 12 points in support of South's opening spade bid and the pair is off. South takes control by making a Blackwood four-no-trump bid, which will be discussed in the next chapter. North's five diamonds shows one ace.

South was sure that the worst he could expect would be that the slam would depend on a finesse. He bid six spades.

West opened and continued hearts. South ruffed the second heart and led the ace of spades. West showed out and with the trumps all in one hand, South had to proceed with caution.

He entered dummy with a second trump, ruffed dummy's last heart and then pulled trumps. Because he had ruffed twice in his own hand, he was able to discard a losing diamond on dummy's last trump. This maneuver is called a dummy reversal play.

The last six tricks were made with top diamonds and clubs.

Slam could probably have been reached in any bidding system, but it was a cinch with the limit jump raise.

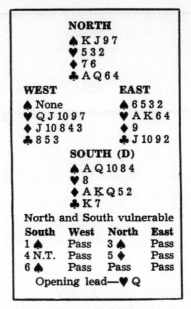

NORTH
♠ K J 9 7
♥ 5 3 2
♦ 7 6
♣ A Q 6 4

WEST
♠ None
♥ Q J 10 9 7
♦ J 10 8 4 3
♣ 8 5 3

EAST
♠ 6 5 3 2
♥ A K 6 4
♦ 9
♣ J 10 9 2

SOUTH (D)
♠ A Q 10 8 4
♥ 8
♦ A K Q 5 2
♣ K 7

North and South vulnerable

South	West	North	East
1 ♠	Pass	3 ♠	Pass
4 N.T.	Pass	5 ♦	Pass
6 ♠	Pass	Pass	Pass

Opening lead—♥ Q

Hand No. 12

After partner makes a response to the opening bidder's call, the next move on the part of the opener depends on his strength and the kind of response his partner has given.

It usually takes 26 points to make a 9-trick game in no-trump or a 10-trick game in a major suit, or 29 points for an 11-trick game in a minor suit.

If partner raises your suit, you revalue your hand upward by adding one point for your fifth trump and two points for each extra trump. His raise has increased the value of your trumps. If he gives a single raise it shows 7 to 10 points in support. If your revalued hand counts 15 or less, pass. 15 plus 10 is only 25. If your suit is a major and your recount shows 16 or 17, bid three and invite four. With 18, bid game. If your minor suit has been raised, you need three points more to act unless you visualize no-trump possibilities.

A forcing jump raise requires that you bid again. A limit jump raise shows 10+ to 13− points and should be passed only if your hand is a bare minimum.

The triple raise shows tremendous distribution and not much in high cards. It has put you in game and you should only go on if you have a lot of high cards.

If your partner responds one no-trump, he shows 7 to 10 points and a balanced hand. With less than 17 points of your own, pass — except that you rebid a six-card suit or bid a second suit if your hand includes a singleton.

If he responds in a new suit at the one level you must rebid, but you should bear in mind that your partner may hold as little as 7 points, so don't head for the stratosphere right away. He may have a good hand, in which case he knows it and will take strong action himself.

If his new suit response is at the two level, he shows at least 10 points and again is forcing for one round.

Usually competition at the bridge table is strong and only the strong bidders get good scores.

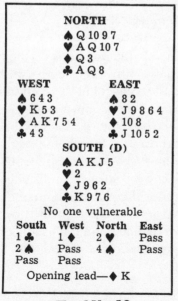

Hand No. 13

In Hand No. 13, sitting in North was Bob Hamman of the

United States World Olympiad team. His partner, in the South seat, was Don Krauss.

After Don's opening club bid and the one diamond overcall, Bob decided he wanted to invite a slam without taking the bidding past game. He therefore served notice by jumping to two hearts as his first bid. This procedure is utterly foreign to the minimum-bid school, but when he followed it by a jump raise to four spades he had managed to get his message across without going past game.

Don got the message, but he also had a minimum hand with a singleton in his partner's suit. Don had no slam interest and passed.

West's opening lead was the king of diamonds. He followed with the ace and a third diamond, which Don ruffed in dummy with the nine-spot.

Don drew trumps and took a heart finesse to make 11 tricks. He decided the finesse was a better gamble than the club break.

The play of this hand looked easy, but it was a big swing for the American team in the Olympiad.

When the opposing team bid the hand against the American East-West, North merely bid one heart on the first round. Later North jumped to three clubs over South's one-spade rebid and went to five spades after South bid three no-trump.

South bid six spades and was down one.

North's aggressiveness came too late in this case and South was swept into an unreasonably high contract.

However, South must shoulder a considerable portion of the blame. His partner had bid strongly and had gone past game all by himself, but South still had a rock-bottom minimum opening bid and he could do nothing about the first two diamond leads. North had indicated that he could not handle diamonds. He had bid hearts, clubs and supported spades, but he had not mentioned diamonds.

3

Many Uses of No-Trump

WE have already discussed no-trump bids that have nothing to do with no-trump. The mention of no-trump in the bidding is very often significant — it may be a probe to learn power for slam, it may show a strong hand, or it may merely indicate that the bidder does not have help in the suit his partner has bid.

But when the bidder opens with one, two or three no-trump he is making a picture bid that tells his partner exactly the kind of hand he has. Partner's response will tell the opener one of three things: (a) stop at once, (b) go on in no-trump if you can, or (c) try to continue in a suit.

All opening no-trump bids must fit definite specifications. They should be of even distribution: 4-3-3-3, or reasonably near. Here are other specifications:

1. No voids, singletons and not more than one doubleton, and that should include a jack or better.
2. At least three suits stopped for an opening bid of one, and all suits stopped for two or more.
3. The bidder must be prepared for the opening lead.
4. The hand must come within certain high-card point limits: 15 to 17 for one no-trump; 21 to 23 for two; 24 to 26 for three.

If you have 13 or 14 points and no-trump shape, open with one of a suit and plan to make a minimum bid in no-trump if your partner shows another suit. With 18 to 20 points, open one of a suit and jump to no-trump later.

There are limits for partner's response to opening no-trump bids. (In this connection, special bids will be discussed in Chapter 6, when we take up the Stayman convention and the Jacoby transfer.)

Partner passes with balanced distribution and less than 9 high-card points after an opening one no-trump bid. If he has a six- or five-carder with a singleton or void, he takes him out in that suit. Unlike other suit bids, this new suit call at the two level (a two-over-one bid) is nonforcing and a sign of weakness. The no-trump bidder usually passes.

With 9 or 10 high-card points, invite game with a raise to two no-trump or force to game by a jump bid in a suit of five cards or more. You can afford to jump with this count because your partner's opening promised at least two cards in each suit.

With 11 to 15 high-card points, raise to three no-trump or jump in a good suit, which forces the original bidder to go on to game.

With 16 or more high-card points, suggest or bid a slam. (Your partner has shown 15 to 17 points, and you need 33 points in both hands for a small slam, 37 for a grand slam.)

If you have bid one no-trump and your partner raises to two, go to game if you have a maximum or near maximum hand.

Any bid made after an opening two no-trump is forcing to game. Therefore if you have less than 4 high-card points, pass. With 4 to 9 high-card points, bid a five- or six-card suit (or longer) if you have unbalanced distribution. If your hand holds 10 or more points, work toward a slam. Make sure you get there if you have 12 or more high-card points.

If your partner bids three no-trump, he has 24 to 26 points; if you respond, you are inviting him to bid a slam. You should therefore pass if you have a bad hand.

If you have opened no-trump and your partner has responded, bid only what is required. You can judge his strength by his response if he does not force you to bid. Do not keep bidding on values you have already announced. If your partner bids two no-trump, bid three if you have a maximum. If he bids two of a suit over your one no-trump, you should generally pass. If he jumps you are forced to rebid — either raise him to game in a major suit if you have three trumps to an honor or any four trumps, or bid three no-trump.

If your partner responds after a two no-trump and you are weak in his suit, bid three no-trump. If you have four trumps, or three trumps with at least one honor, you can go on to game, or you can bid a new suit if you want to suggest a slam.

In Hand No. 14, which was played by Ira Rubin, an outstanding expert, the opening was made with a typical no-trump distribution and 16 high-card points. Ira's partner, North, with 11 high-card points, went directly to game.

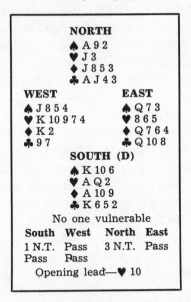

Hand No. 14

Some of the most instructive bridge hands look elementary when you watch an expert play them, and this one was no exception.

Ira covered the opening lead of the ten of hearts with dummy's jack. When it held, he led a diamond and finessed the nine. West took his king and made his best return — the nine of clubs.

Ira went right up with dummy's ace and finessed the diamond again. This time it worked and he cashed the ace of diamonds, hoping the queen would drop, but it did not. Then Ira went after clubs and wound up with two spades, two hearts, two diamonds and three clubs.

It looked simple, but let's study Ira's reasons for adopting this line of play.

Why did he play second hand high at trick one? Because he could derive no benefit from the jack of hearts if he did not play it then and there.

Why did he attack diamonds instead of clubs at trick two? Because he did not want to let East into the lead and an unsuccessful club finesse would put the lead in the East hand.

Why did he go right up with dummy's ace of clubs at trick three? Because he wanted the lead in dummy, not in his own hand, and because he was certain that West had not led from the queen of clubs.

Why did he take the second diamond finesse? Because if he lost no damage would result. West would be back in the lead and he would have nothing good to play.

Undoubtedly the team of four match is the greatest test of bridge skill. But there is an opportunity for a lot of good luck also. We will discuss tournament bridge later on, but Hand No. 15 is a good example of no-trump bidding and play.

At the first table the bidding proceeded as shown in the diagram. South, with 19 points and a balanced hand, went to two no-trump after his partner responded one spade to the opening diamond bid. South had stoppers in all suits except spades and his partner had shown strength in that suit. The bidding continued till a small-slam contract was reached.

Although the bidding went along the lines of that discussed

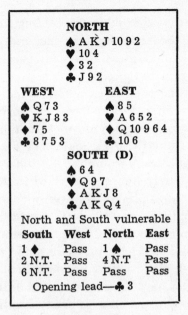

NORTH
♠ A K J 10 9 2
♥ 10 4
♦ 3 2
♣ J 9 2

WEST
♠ Q 7 3
♥ K J 8 3
♦ 7 5
♣ 8 7 5 3

EAST
♠ 8 5
♥ A 6 5 2
♦ Q 10 9 6 4
♣ 10 6

SOUTH (D)
♠ 6 4
♥ Q 9 7
♦ A K J 8
♣ A K Q 4

North and South vulnerable

South	West	North	East
1 ♦	Pass	1 ♠	Pass
2 N.T.	Pass	4 N.T	Pass
6 N.T.	Pass	Pass	Pass

Opening lead—♣ 3

Hand No. 15

in this chapter, in some circles South would have bid three clubs instead of two no-trump, which would show his strength more clearly. In that event North probably would have bid four spades instead of four no-trump, which would be a move toward slam. But in any event, the slam was not a safe one, as we can see by glancing at the cards.

Let's see what happened.

West had to make a lead and he decided that a heart opening would be likely to cost an important trick. So he opened a safe club.

Declarer won the trick in his hand, took the spade finesse and then ran off all 13 tricks after East unguarded his queen of diamonds.

The only comment we will make on West's opening lead is to quote the man himself:

"If I held this hand next week or next year, I still wouldn't lead a heart!"

However, at the other table the bidding went approximately the same way at the beginning: one diamond, one spade, two no-trump, four no-trump. But at this point, South saw no particular reason to bid again and passed.

The West at this table liked to attack and he did not have a trauma about leading from a king-jack tenace. He opened the three of hearts and the defense took four heart tricks before South could get into the lead. South took the rest of the tricks, but down one at four no-trump is never a happy result.

The four no-trump bidding described in the above hand was not Blackwood. Most players today consider that any bid of four no-trump is a call for aces. However, some do not use the Blackwood convention if there has been a no-trump bid previously. But Blackwood, if used here, probably would not have made any difference. South made a risky bid of six no-trump *hoping* that his partner would have the ace or king of hearts.

The Blackwood convention is pretty familiar territory to all bridge players. It is a four no-trump bid after a showing of strength in the partnership, and it simply says: "Partner, how many aces have you?"

Most new conventions are adopted by experts first, then by writers and teachers, and finally by rank-and-file players. But although Easley Blackwood of Indianapolis, the creator of the convention, is an expert, his idea was first accepted by the great mass of bridge players while other experts held aloof for a long time. Even today some experts try to avoid using the convention.

Of course there are some hands that aren't suitable for Blackwood, but unless you can count enough strength to warrant a slam bid all by yourself, unless you are void in any suit and you hold two quick losers in a suit bid by your opponents, it is downright silly not to check for aces via Blackwood as a precautionary measure before going into a slam contract.

Go back to Hand No. 13 briefly. Bob Hamman recognized slam possibilities, but he managed to get the slam idea across without jeopardizing game by his two jump bids. When you have enough strength so that you see a slam possibility, provided your opponents can't take the first two tricks, you use Blackwood as a check for aces.

Don't use Blackwood until you can count enough strength for the slam. It is more of a safety check than anything else. And don't use Blackwood unless you plan to go on to the slam if your side holds three of the four aces.

When your partner fails to use Blackwood but does bid beyond game, try to figure out his reason. You bid one spade. He responds two hearts and you jump to four hearts. At this point he bids five clubs.

Why? Since he has gone past game, he is trying for a slam. He isn't trying to find a better suit, because you have supported hearts enthusiastically. He must be afraid of diamonds. If you can handle the first diamond you should bid five diamonds to tell him about it. If you can handle the second diamond you should jump to six hearts. If you have two diamond losers you should merely bid five hearts irrespective of the rest of your hand.

Before you use Blackwood you should know where you are going. Don't use it until you know that you can play in no-trump or in some specific suit. In other words, don't hunt lions with a shotgun.

Your responses to a Blackwood four no-trump are: five clubs with no aces or four aces; five diamonds with one; five hearts with two; five spades with three.

The five-club response to show no aces or four aces should cause no confusion. If you can't tell from your own hand and the previous bidding the difference between four aces and no aces you shouldn't be playing bridge.

If all aces are accounted for in your hand and your partner's, the follow-up bid of five no-trump is a demand for partner to tell how many kings he holds. Again: none, six clubs; one, six diamonds, two, six hearts, three, six spades. However, *if you have all four kings, bid six no-trump.*

Hand No. 16 shows the advantage of using the five-club response to show four aces. If five no-trump were bid to show four aces, there would be no satisfactory way to ask for kings in the event a grand slam was in sight.

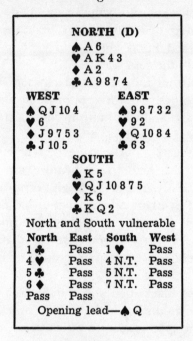

NORTH (D)
♠ A 6
♥ A K 4 3
♦ A 2
♣ A 9 8 7 4

WEST
♠ Q J 10 4
♥ 6
♦ J 9 7 5 3
♣ J 10 5

EAST
♠ 9 8 7 3 2
♥ 9 2
♦ Q 10 8 4
♣ 6 3

SOUTH
♠ K 5
♥ Q J 10 8 7 5
♦ K 6
♣ K Q 2

North and South vulnerable

North	East	South	West
1 ♣	Pass	1 ♥	Pass
4 ♥	Pass	4 N.T.	Pass
5 ♣	Pass	5 N.T.	Pass
6 ♦	Pass	7 N.T.	Pass
Pass	Pass		

Opening lead—♠ Q

Hand No. 16

Look at the bidding: North opens one club. After South responds one heart, North goes immediately to four hearts. From this South knows that North will show up with at least one ace, because he would need that much to open the bidding. So South bids four no-trump. Now North responds five clubs and South is certain that all four aces are in his partner's hand.

The next step is to go on to grand slam if possible. Now the king of hearts becomes a very important card. If North holds this card a grand slam is certain. The bid of five no-trump is open, because North responded five clubs to show all the aces. If five no-trump were the response for all the aces, South would have had no way to find out about the king of hearts and would have had to guess whether to bid seven or settle for a sure six.

North responds six diamonds to South's five no-trump. This shows one king and since South holds the other three he is able to bid seven with certainty of success. He also bids it in no-trump since there are thirteen tricks there also.

In the early 'thirties, before Blackwood was invented, Hand No. 17 would probably never have been bid to a grand slam.

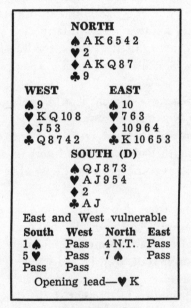

NORTH
♠ A K 6 5 4 2
♥ 2
♦ A K Q 8 7
♣ 9

WEST
♠ 9
♥ K Q 10 8
♦ J 5 3
♣ Q 8 7 4 2

EAST
♠ 10
♥ 7 6 3
♦ 10 9 6 4
♣ K 10 6 5 3

SOUTH (D)
♠ Q J 8 7 3
♥ A J 9 5 4
♦ 2
♣ A J

East and West vulnerable

South	West	North	East
1 ♠	Pass	4 N.T.	Pass
5 ♥	Pass	7 ♠	Pass
Pass	Pass		

Opening lead—♥ K

Hand No. 17

In those days, an expert playing in the North seat undoubtedly would have responded three diamonds after his partner opened with one spade. After South bid three hearts, North would have jumped to six spades. In those days no one could do any better with the bidding tools at hand.

Today, even students learning the game would have no trouble reaching seven spades. North has a perfect hand for Blackwood because he can stop at five if his partner has opened without an ace. He can settle for six if his partner shows one ace or bid the grand slam with safety if his partner shows two.

By 1934 various methods of asking for aces were being tried. Today Blackwood and Gerber are the only two in wide use. Gerber will be discussed in Chapter 7.

Every hand, as we said, is not suited for Blackwood. And there are pitfalls to avoid.

In Hand No. 18, when North opened with a heart, South, with 18 high-card points, could easily assume that there was enough strength in the two hands to explore slam possibilities. South immediately made a jump-shift to two spades, which is forcing to game. North raised to three spades, thus establishing the suit, and now South had to decide a couple of important questions.

If South used Blackwood, what would he do if North showed two aces? What if North showed only one ace?

In this case there was no satisfactory answer to either question. As you can see, South had two quick losers in diamonds and if his partner had no aces there would be trouble in that suit.

But South found what appeared to be a good way to invite the slam without using Blackwood. He bid four clubs.

North, who had only a minimum opening with 13 high-card points and two doubletons, showed his strength in hearts by re-bidding in that suit.

South then bid five spades. This bid clearly drew a diagram for North. It told him that he must take care of the first or second diamond lead if they went after the slam. North could not; and he therefore passed at five spades, which was all that could be made with the hand.

Two Blackwood "don'ts" are evident from this illustration:

1. Don't use Blackwood when you hold a worthless doubleton in an unbid suit.

2. Don't use Blackwood when you are not prepared to bid a slam if your partner's response shows that your side has three of the four aces.

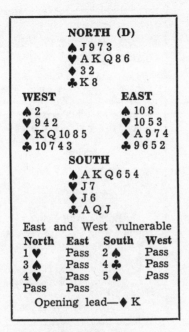

NORTH (D)
♠ J 9 7 3
♥ A K Q 8 6
♦ 3 2
♣ K 8

WEST
♠ 2
♥ 9 4 2
♦ K Q 10 8 5
♣ 10 7 4 3

EAST
♠ 10 8
♥ 10 5 3
♦ A 9 7 4
♣ 9 6 5 2

SOUTH
♠ A K Q 6 5 4
♥ J 7
♦ J 6
♣ A Q J

East and West vulnerable

North	East	South	West
1 ♥	Pass	2 ♠	Pass
3 ♠	Pass	4 ♣	Pass
4 ♥	Pass	5 ♠	Pass
Pass	Pass		

Opening lead—♦ K

Hand No. 18

Experts are in complete agreement as to the meaning of most bids in Blackwood sequences. There are, on the other hand, different opinions on what to do when your partner uses Blackwood and you have a void.

The Jacoby method, which we naturally endorse, is to decide first whether the void is a "good" one. That is, will it help make the slam? If it is, we *jump to six in the suit that shows the number of aces* we actually hold.

In Hand No. 19, North has two aces and a void. Diamonds have not been bid and the void is obviously "good." Spades have been established as the suit in which the slam will be played and when South bids the Blackwood four no-trump, North must show his aces.

But in order to show the void, North bids six hearts, showing that he has two aces and a void. (It is just coincidental that

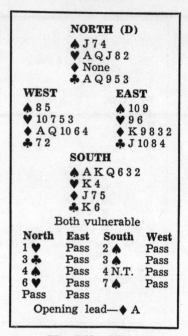

Hand No. 19

North also has good hearts, since he knows South will return to spades.)

The jump solves all South's problems. He can bid seven spades with full assurance that he will be in a winning contract, barring something like a first-round ruff.

When you show a void in this manner, be sure that you do not force your partner to bid beyond six in the agreed trump suit. Another word of caution: be sure your partner understands this bid.

On this hand, it may appear that South took a chance when he went into Blackwood, in view of the possibility that North might hold two small diamonds. South did take that chance, but it was not a big risk because North had bid hearts and clubs and had raised spades. It was likely that North had a singleton or void in diamonds.

If you use *any* four no-trump as Blackwood, you will sometimes ask for aces after you or your partner has bid no-trump at a lower level. The response given may show that your side will not make slam, but you still want to play the contract in no-trump, rather than in a suit. If you sign off at five no-trump, your partner will mistake the bid as a Blackwood call for kings and show them at the six level.

The proper procedure in this case is to bid five in a previously unbid suit, which requests your partner to sign off at five no-trump, which then becomes the final contract.

For example, the bidding might be: One club; *two no-trump*; three hearts; *three no-trump*; four no-trump; *five clubs*; five spades; *five no-trump*. (In this sequence, passes of your opponents have been omitted and your partner's bids are in italics.) Your five-spade bid simply said: "Partner, we lack aces, so please sign off in no-trump."

The Jacoby system is to use the Blackwood convention when appropriate, but we can easily spot times when it is best not to use it.

Hand No. 20 illustrates one of these occasions. South has a perfect hand for not using Blackwood. But he used it anyway and Blackwooded himself right out of a slam.

South could gain no information of any real value by using the Blackwood convention with this hand. If North showed an ace, South would not be strong enough to try for seven. If North showed no ace, South was afraid to bid six with that worthless doubleton in diamonds and lack of solidarity in the other three suits. North, of course, had no idea how many aces South held and could not bid the slam himself.

In this case South had an easy way to reach slam without using Blackwood. After his partner gave a jump in spades, thus establishing the suit, South could have bid four clubs. This would show slam interest, and give North a chance to sign off in spades if he did not think slam was probable.

However, North would have slam ideas. With his five-card support for spades and second-round control in the other three

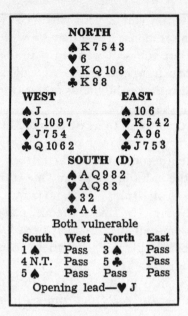

NORTH
♠ K 7 5 4 3
♥ 6
♦ K Q 10 8
♣ K 9 8

WEST
♠ J
♥ J 10 9 7
♦ J 7 5 4
♣ Q 10 6 2

EAST
♠ 10 6
♥ K 5 4 2
♦ A 9 6
♣ J 7 5 3

SOUTH (D)
♠ A Q 9 8 2
♥ A Q 8 3
♦ 3 2
♣ A 4

Both vulnerable

South	West	North	East
1 ♠	Pass	3 ♠	Pass
4 N.T.	Pass	5 ♣	Pass
5 ♠	Pass	Pass	Pass

Opening lead—♥ J

Hand No. 20

suits, North could bid a Blackwood four no-trump. South would respond five spades, to show his three aces, and North would feel secure in bidding six. As the cards show, the slam is there.

Hand No. 21 is a simple little slam. Simple, that is, in expert circles. It shows the best use of the Blackwood convention.

After North showed support for the heart suit, South made the four no-trump call. North showed one ace with his five diamond bid. South's five no-trump guaranteed all the aces in the two hands.

At this point, if North had held additional values, such as the queen of hearts and a real club suit, he would have been entitled to bid seven hearts without delay. But when North bid six hearts to show two kings, South knew that there were some missing queens and settled for the small slam, even though his side held every ace and king.

This hand was played in the International Championship

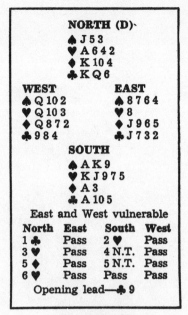

NORTH (D)
♠ J 5 3
♥ A 6 4 2
♦ K 10 4
♣ K Q 6

WEST
♠ Q 10 2
♥ Q 10 3
♦ Q 8 7 2
♣ 9 8 4

EAST
♠ 8 7 6 4
♥ 8
♦ J 9 6 5
♣ J 7 3 2

SOUTH
♠ A K 9
♥ K J 9 7 5
♦ A 3
♣ A 10 5

East and West vulnerable

North	East	South	West
1 ♣	Pass	2 ♥	Pass
3 ♥	Pass	4 N.T.	Pass
5 ♦	Pass	5 N.T.	Pass
6 ♥	Pass	Pass	Pass

Opening lead—♣ 9

Hand No. 21

match between the United States and Italian teams. At both tables the North-South hands bid six hearts and both declarers had no difficulty in making the contract.

The nine of clubs was opened and South played out his ace and king of hearts to learn that there was a sure loser in the trump suit.

Undismayed, South played his ace of diamonds, led a small diamond to dummy's king. Then he ruffed dummy's last diamond and ran off the last two clubs.

Finally he threw West in with the queen of trumps and West had to lead either a spade or a diamond. If West led a diamond he would give South a ruff and the opportunity to discard his losing spade. If West led a spade, he would allow South a free finesse against the spade queen.

The play was so standard for the experts that both declarers played it exactly the same way.

4

Gallant Defenders

ALTHOUGH it is advantageous to open the bidding, it is not always a player's privilege to do so. When an opponent opens the bidding you are on the defensive and you will try your best to defeat him, if he is the successful bidder, or take the bid away from him if you can.

You do not have to bid after your opponents open, and you should not unless you have a good reason. Starting a campaign to enable you or your partner to become the declarer is an adequate reason, or you may simply suggest the best line of defense against an expected adverse contract.

The two methods of getting into the act are the overcall and the takeout double.

An overcall is not the same as an opening bid, and it has different basic requirements. An opening bid requires at least 11 high-card points, but the first requirement for an overcall is a suit strong enough to protect you against a loss of more than 500 points if you are doubled (down two vulnerable, or three not vulnerable).

As an opening bidder you may bid a three-card minor or a four-card major, but you seldom overcall unless you have a five-card suit. Most players never overcall with anything less.

There is no point in making an overcall with a minor suit unless you can take a lot of tricks if it becomes trump. Hence, you don't overcall with a minor unless you have a six-card suit, or in rare cases a *good* five-card suit.

Major-suit overcalls, particularly spades, offer promise because with the top-ranking suit you can compete at a low level.

One of the best bidding tools for the defense is a takeout double, the double of an opponent's bid that asks your partner to "take me out," or bid from his hand. Since the rules of Contract Bridge permit the use of only the word "double" without a qualifying adjective, rigid conventions must be set so that one partner will know what the other means when he doubles — whether it means to bid, or the double is for business.

Here are the basic rules:

1. Any double after the partner has made any call other than a pass is for business.

2. A double of a bid of two no-trump or more, or of a suit bid of four or more, is for business.

3. Any delayed double is for business. (A delayed double is one that is not made at the first opportunity. For example, if your opponent opens a spade and you pass, any later (delayed) double will be for business.)

4. Any double of a bid of one no-trump, or a bid of one, two or three of a suit, made at the doubler's first opportunity, is for takeout provided that the doubler's partner has not previously bid or doubled.

5. Any repeat of a takeout double is still for takeout. Thus, if your opponent bids one spade and you double for takeout, and the opponent's partner bids two spades and your partner and opener pass, a second double by you is still for takeout.

6. To make a takeout double, you should have the equivalent of an opening bid in high-card points (11 or more).

7. You should have a short holding in the suit you double, the shorter the better.

8. You should be able to support any suit bid by your partner or to bid a strong suit of your own.

For a second takeout double (condition 5), requirements vary with the nature of the doubler's hand. With a void or singleton in the doubled suit, not much extra strength is needed. With a doubleton, he needs two or three extra points to justify his repeating his request for his partner to bid. With 4-3-3-3 distribution, a player should practically never repeat his takeout double.

There is one point to remember when you make a takeout double. *You have forced your partner to bid and he may have a bust hand.*

If your partner doubles, you must show him strength if you can. Do not pass with a bad hand merely because you are afraid of being set. Your duty is to bid your best suit. The weaker your hand, the more important it is for you to bid. If, however, you have a strong holding in your opponent's suit you may think you will be able to set him. In this case your pass indicates strength, not weakness. You pass a takeout double for penalties only. Do not pass if you have a long but shabby holding — pass only if you are strong in your opponent's bid. You must develop three tricks or more in trumps.

Here are the requirements for a response:

With 0 to 8 points, make a minimum bid and plan to pass unless your partner continues with another strong bid.

With 9 or 10 points, strain for a game contract. Jump if you possibly can. With a stopper in the opponents' suit, bid one no-trump.

With 11 or more points make a jump bid of some kind or bid the opponents' suit to show your strength.

What you do if your partner makes a minimum response to your takeout double depends upon your strength. You have forced him to bid and since his minimum response does not show much strength:

With 11 to 14 points in high cards, pass.

15 to 17 high-card points, give a single raise if you have good trumps. Partner will rebid with 9 or 10 points.

18-20 high-card points, give a jump raise.

21-23 high-card points, bid game.

Hand No. 22 shows the use of both the penalty and takeout double. It was played by Besse and Durouvenoz of Switzerland against one of the few pairs who used the weak no-trump in the World Bridge Olympiad in 1964.

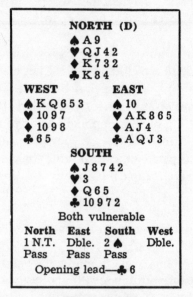

NORTH (D)
♠ A 9
♥ Q J 4 2
♦ K 7 3 2
♣ K 8 4

WEST
♠ K Q 6 5 3
♥ 10 9 7
♦ 10 9 8
♣ 6 5

EAST
♠ 10
♥ A K 8 6 5
♦ A J 4
♣ A Q J 3

SOUTH
♠ J 8 7 4 2
♥ 3
♦ Q 6 5
♣ 10 9 7 2

Both vulnerable

North	East	South	West
1 N.T.	Dble.	2 ♠	Dble.
Pass	Pass	Pass	

Opening lead—♣ 6

Hand No. 22

South saw no reason to stay in one no-trump doubled, so he ran out to two spades, which turned out no better.

Besse (East) won his partner's opening club lead with his jack and led back the ten of trumps. South's jack was allowed to hold the trick and he led his singleton heart. North's jack fell under East's king and East got out of the trap by playing the ace and another club which Durouvenoz, sitting West, trumped. West returned his remaining small trump and dummy was in with the ace.

A low diamond was led from dummy and after East ducked, South took the trick with his queen. South now had three tricks and he threw Besse in with his last club. West discarded a heart. Besse appeared to be end-played but he got out by leading the ace of hearts for South to ruff. This was South's fourth and last trick. He was left with two low trumps and two low diamonds, while West held two high trumps and East two high diamonds behind dummy's king. South was down four tricks for a minus 1,100 points.

In this example East's takeout double showed a very strong hand. You do not make a takeout double over a no-trump without the high-card count equivalent to a no-trump opening. Therefore West felt that he was entitled to make a business double with his long spades.

Hand No. 23 shows a strong response to a takeout double and the eventual bidding of a slam.

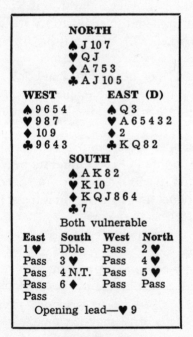

NORTH
♠ J 10 7
♥ Q J
♦ A 7 5 3
♣ A J 10 5

WEST
♠ 9 6 5 4
♥ 9 8 7
♦ 10 9
♣ 9 6 4 3

EAST (D)
♠ Q 3
♥ A 6 5 4 3 2
♦ 2
♣ K Q 8 2

SOUTH
♠ A K 8 2
♥ K 10
♦ K Q J 8 6 4
♣ 7

Both vulnerable

East	South	West	North
1 ♥	Dble	Pass	2 ♥
Pass	3 ♥	Pass	4 ♥
Pass	4 N.T.	Pass	5 ♥
Pass	6 ♦	Pass	Pass
Pass			

Opening lead—♥ 9

Hand No. 23

The hand was played by Bobby Jordan and Arthur Robinson against Barry Crane and Oswald Jacoby in the U.S. team trials for the World's Championship in Dallas, Texas, late in 1964.

It was tournament competition and every East player opened with one heart and in each case South either doubled or bid two diamonds. With his hand Arthur, sitting South, doubled and Bobby bid two hearts to show great strength. Arthur bid three hearts in an effort to get Bobby to spades, but Bobby had only three spades, hence his four-heart call.

This bid clearly told Arthur to choose a minor suit and his obvious choice was diamonds, but Arthur had a better bid at his disposal in a four no-trump Blackwood.

If Bobby had one ace, he would respond five diamonds and Arthur would pass. If Bobby held two aces, Arthur would bid six. The latter case held.

The hand would have been a laydown if North had held only two spades. As it was, South needed to try the spade finesse but since East was marked with every missing high card, the finesse was a sure thing.

In Hand No. 24, look at the East hand only. You are vulnerable. South who is not vulnerable opens three hearts. West doubles and North jumps to six hearts. What would you do?

For all you know, you and your partner may be cold for six spades, but you should not expect to set six hearts by very much. On the other hand, no bridge player can expect the maximum result on every hand, and if he is going to be fixed, at least he wants to be fixed with a plus score.

Hence the best answer the Jacobys can give is to double and take the sure plus.

This hand came up in a tournament at New Rochelle, New York, and for once good bidding was rewarded. Six spades would have been down one. Six hearts went down four tricks so that the double gave East and West a top score.

North's jump to six hearts is the type of bid known as a premature save, which is a hazardous undertaking. What East would have done if North had been a trifle less sensational and merely jumped to five hearts, no one will ever know. But if East doubles five hearts he winds up only 500 points plus, which is a

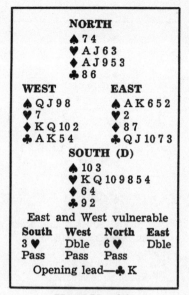

NORTH
♠ 7 4
♥ A J 6 3
♦ A J 9 5 3
♣ 8 6

WEST
♠ Q J 9 8
♥ 7
♦ K Q 10 2
♣ A K 5 4

EAST
♠ A K 6 5 2
♥ 2
♦ 8 7
♣ Q J 10 7 3

SOUTH (D)
♠ 10 3
♥ K Q 10 9 8 5 4
♦ 6 4
♣ 9 2

East and West vulnerable

South	West	North	East
3 ♥	Dble	6 ♥	Dble
Pass	Pass	Pass	

Opening lead—♣ K

Hand No. 24

bad score, considering that he would have made five spades vulnerable. But if East bids five spades he is taking a chance. And if he does bid five, his partner may go on to six.

You could speculate on a hand like this all night. In Hand No. 25, West could hardly believe his ears when South made his two-spade overcall. But his astonishment did not keep him from doubling for business.

You will note that this could not be mistaken for a takeout double.

South had no place to seek shelter and he watched West play his king and ace of hearts and queen and another club. East took his ace and king of clubs, then shifted to a trump, which West won with the ten.

West played the ace and four of diamonds. East's king of diamonds became the eighth defensive trick and a third diamond ruffed by West was the ninth. And there was still another trump to lose.

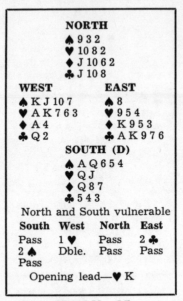

NORTH
♠ 9 3 2
♥ 10 8 2
♦ J 10 6 2
♣ J 10 8

WEST
♠ K J 10 7
♥ A K 7 6 3
♦ A 4
♣ Q 2

EAST
♠ 8
♥ 9 5 4
♦ K 9 5 3
♣ A K 9 7 6

SOUTH (D)
♠ A Q 6 5 4
♥ Q J
♦ Q 8 7
♣ 5 4 3

North and South vulnerable

South	West	North	East
Pass	1 ♥	Pass	2 ♣
2 ♠	Dble.	Pass	Pass
Pass			

Opening lead—♥ K

Hand No. 25

South told his partner that he had saved a slam, but he had not. East and West could come close, but close doesn't count. South mentioned his 11 high-card points, plus a doubleton, but this was no alibi. Seven of the points were in queens and jacks and he had no right to expect them to take many tricks.

Points don't take tricks. Cards do.

When you make a business double, be sure that there are enough cards in your hand and your partner's to set your opponents. Appearances are sometimes deceptive, as illustrated in Hand No. 26.

The hand, which was played by Chuck Berger of Detroit in the Toledo regionals in 1965, probably established some kind of record for making potential tricks disappear.

At first sight of the dummy, Chuck knew he had a tough contract to bring home, since he could be certain West had doubled on long trumps. But that knowledge turned out to be power.

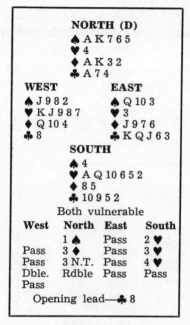

NORTH (D)
♠ A K 7 6 5
♥ 4
♦ A K 3 2
♣ A 7 4

WEST
♠ J 9 8 2
♥ K J 9 8 7
♦ Q 10 4
♣ 8

EAST
♠ Q 10 3
♥ 3
♦ J 9 7 6
♣ K Q J 6 3

SOUTH
♠ 4
♥ A Q 10 6 5 2
♦ 8 5
♣ 10 9 5 2

Both vulnerable

West	North	East	South
	1 ♠	Pass	2 ♥
Pass	3 ♦	Pass	3 ♥
Pass	3 N.T.	Pass	4 ♥
Dble.	Rdble	Pass	Pass
Pass			

Opening lead—♣ 8

Hand No. 26

West opened his singleton club and Chuck cashed his ace and king of spades after taking the first trick. He discarded a club on the second spade lead. Then he ruffed a spade and returned to the dummy with the king of diamonds. He ruffed another spade and West had to follow suit. Then he played the ace of diamonds and ruffed a diamond.

At this point Chuck had taken eight tricks, the opponents none. He held the ace, queen and ten of trumps and two losing clubs. He led a low club and now West's five trumps became a liability. He had to trump his partner's trick and lead back a heart, which Chuck captured with his ten. Back went another club and again West was in the lead. West had to concede the last two tricks to Chuck's ace and queen of trumps.

Hand No. 27 illustrates a good defensive problem for both sides of the table. East had a good opening bid, with a club suit and support for both majors, but South gave a jump overcall with a six-card spade suit. South was Dick Walsh of Los Angeles, and East was another expert. After North sewed up the contract with a bid of four spades, West led a low club.

In ordinary competition, East would win the club with the ace and return the queen, and from that point on, declarer would have no trouble making his contract. But East, being an expert, played the jack of clubs, and when it held, East was ready for a neat defensive trick.

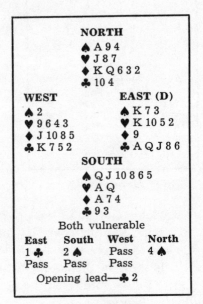

NORTH
♠ A 9 4
♥ J 8 7
♦ K Q 6 3 2
♣ 10 4

WEST
♠ 2
♥ 9 6 4 3
♦ J 10 8 5
♣ K 7 5 2

EAST (D)
♠ K 7 3
♥ K 10 5 2
♦ 9
♣ A Q J 8 6

SOUTH
♠ Q J 10 8 6 5
♥ A Q
♦ A 7 4
♣ 9 3

Both vulnerable

East	South	West	North
1 ♣	2 ♠	Pass	4 ♠
Pass	Pass	Pass	

Opening lead—♣ 2

Hand No. 27

He led his singleton diamond. He planned to take his king of trumps at the first opportunity and throw his partner in with the king of clubs, whereupon a diamond ruff would send South to the showers.

However, Dick Walsh saw what East was up to and foiled this plot. Dick had to keep West out of the lead. He won the diamond in dummy and took the heart finesse. Then he cashed his ace of hearts, returned to dummy with the ace of trumps and led the jack of hearts. East played the king, and Dick discarded his remaining club — a play called loser-on-loser.

East now was in the lead with no way to get to his partner's hand. East led another club, of course, hoping that the discard was a false-card, but Dick ruffed, gave East his king of trumps and racked up the rubber.

Another defense tactic is sacrifice bidding. We already showed a type of this in Hand No. 24, and it will be discussed later. Usually, however, sacrifices do not go quite so high, or suffer such a severe penalty.

We do believe in sacrifice bidding, which is called "flag flying" by most of those who play a lot of bridge.

Sacrifice bids incur a double hazard. The first is that you may be jousting with windmills, to learn later, after the other side chalks up several hundred points, that you made a serious mistake. In other words, you could have made a profit by passing and setting them. The second hazard is that the penalty will be too much, even though you have prevented your opponents from making game and rubber.

On the other side of the ledger, a sacrifice bid can occasionally achieve a real success. Often your opponents will disdain the penalty and bid one more only to find that the extra trick is unattainable.

In Hand No. 28, West had a fine spade overcall. He held back over South's three-heart rebid but did bid four spades after North raised to four hearts.

North doubled. He had a probable spade trick — (very probable, it might be said), the ace of diamonds, the king of clubs — and his partner had opened the bidding.

Had South passed, West would have suffered a 500-point penalty. No one enjoys taking such sets, but West would have saved game, rubber and 100 honors, since this was a rubber bridge game.

However, South did not like to have his honors taken away and went on to five hearts. Now the save really paid off for West,

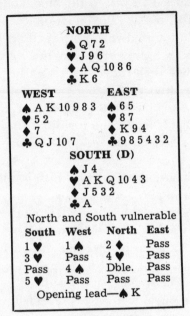

NORTH
♠ Q 7 2
♥ J 9 6
♦ A Q 10 8 6
♣ K 6

WEST
♠ A K 10 9 8 3
♥ 5 2
♦ 7
♣ Q J 10 7

EAST
♠ 6 5
♥ 8 7
♦ K 9 4
♣ 9 8 5 4 3 2

SOUTH (D)
♠ J 4
♥ A K Q 10 4 3
♦ J 5 3 2
♣ A

North and South vulnerable

South	West	North	East
1 ♥	1 ♠	2 ♦	Pass
3 ♥	Pass	4 ♥	Pass
Pass	4 ♠	Dble.	Pass
5 ♥	Pass	Pass	Pass

Opening lead—♠ K

Hand No. 28

who opened the king of spades. East echoed with the six. South false-carded futilely with the jack, but West played the ace. Later East made his king of diamonds and South's potential profits went to never-never land.

5

You, the Aggressor

NO matter where you sit at the table, you and your partner are the good guys and your opponents are the bad guys. You use every bidding and playing tool at your disposal to defeat the bad guys and you must remember that timid bidders and players do not finish on top.

Quite often you will find a hand that is skimpy in honor count, (that is, it has less than the 11 points needed for a very minimum opening), but that has a long suit. So you make a shut-out bid, which is sometimes known under the fancy name of preemptive.

This is an opening bid of three or four, designed to shut the bad guys out of the bidding. Failing in that objective, it is intended to crowd the bidding so that the bad guys cannot arrive at their best contract.

Here are the general requirements for a hand on which you can make a shutout bid:

A strong suit of at least six cards, usually more.

Not more than four points in high cards *outside* of your strong suit.

Enough playing tricks in your own hand to put you within two tricks of your bid, if vulnerable, or within three tricks of your bid if not vulnerable. This means that you should not be set more than 500 points if your partner holds a bust and you are doubled.

63

Preemptive bidding is unnecessary when you have a strong defensive hand. Let the opponents bid. For example, a long suit plus a few of the top honors and an outside entry can often defeat a no-trump game.

If your opponents get too far out of line there is often much more profit in doubling than you can make by trying to bring home a doubtful contract.

Therefore a preemptive bid is made when your strength is concentrated in one long suit and in good distribution otherwise, rather than in high cards.

Slam is normally out of reach after an opening preemptive bid. If your partner makes a preemptive bid, he is telling you that his hand is no good unless the suit he names is trump. Unless you have first-round control of at least two of the other suits and at least second-round control of the third, you should not even think of a slam. An ample supply of aces, kings and queens are necessary to assure the required number of tricks. Your partner has guaranteed only enough tricks to come within two or three of his contract.

If your partner makes a shutout at one less than game, you are justified in raising to game if you have three quick tricks in high cards. Distribution points are of little or no value without trump support.

When your partner makes a minor-suit shutout at the three level, you have a problem. Many times the hand will make three no-trump, and five of the minor suit is an impossible contract. The best rule to follow in this case is that if you have three or more quick tricks in high cards, including stoppers in all three of the unbid suits, bid three no-trump. If your partner's hand is not suitable for a sporting three no-trump, he will bid four or five in his minor-suit holding.

South has a very good preemptive bid on Hand No. 29, with an eight-card spade suit and three points outside. His hand is not strong enough in high cards to open at the one level and even if he loses the king of spades he can see seven or eight probable tricks.

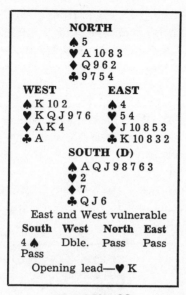

NORTH
♠ 5
♥ A 10 8 3
♦ Q 9 6 2
♣ 9 7 5 4

WEST
♠ K 10 2
♥ K Q J 9 7 6
♦ A K 4
♣ A

EAST
♠ 4
♥ 5 4
♦ J 10 8 5 3
♣ K 10 8 3 2

SOUTH (D)
♠ A Q J 9 8 7 6 3
♥ 2
♦ 7
♣ Q J 6

East and West vulnerable

South	West	North	East
4 ♠	Dble.	Pass	Pass
Pass			

Opening lead—♥ K

Hand No. 29

Now put yourself in the West seat. You sort your cards, enjoying the technicolor of 20 high-card points and a six-card heart suit. You have been trying to decide whether to open with a conservative one-heart or an optimistic two.

Either prospect is pleasing, but you are suddenly brought back from unreality by South's bid of four spades, instead of passing like an agreeable opponent is expected to do. How do you solve the problem?

You will note a similarity here with Hand No. 24, where you were sitting East and the bidding got to six before you had a chance to remind anyone you were a fourth at bridge. However, this is somewhat different. South has a legitimate bid, and in that hand North's bid was somewhat questionable.

This bid has done exactly what a shutout should do. It has thrown confusion into the enemy by putting the bidding too high for the person with high cards to get into the action. Besides, you (East-West) are vulnerable and North-South is not.

Thirty years ago, Oswald Jacoby would have bid five hearts.

All that he would need in his partner's hand would be heart support, the queen of diamonds and a singleton spade. Ozzie would have been determined not to let South steal the hand.

But after thirty years of being fixed by everyone from the greatest experts to the veriest beginners, he would double today.

The theory, we repeat, is that when you expect to be fixed, try to get a plus score. West has a good chance to set South, who admittedly has nothing but a spade suit, and there is nothing sure about five hearts. As you can see by the cards, it is the right decision in this case.

Hand No. 30 was picked up by Orin E. (Babe) Hollingberry, retired football coach of Washington State, an avid bridge player.

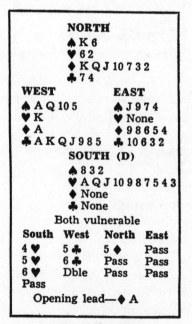

NORTH
♠ K 6
♥ 6 2
♦ K Q J 10 7 3 2
♣ 7 4

WEST
♠ A Q 10 5
♥ K
♦ A
♣ A K Q J 9 8 5

EAST
♠ J 9 7 4
♥ None
♦ 9 8 6 5 4
♣ 10 6 3 2

SOUTH (D)
♠ 8 3 2
♥ A Q J 10 9 8 7 5 4 3
♦ None
♣ None

Both vulnerable

South	West	North	East
4 ♥	5 ♣	5 ♦	Pass
5 ♥	6 ♣	Pass	Pass
6 ♥	Dble	Pass	Pass
Pass			

Opening lead—♦ A

Hand No. 30

Like any football player, Babe used straight power through the line with his ten-card heart suit. Even if the king of hearts did not turn up as a singleton in an opponent's hand, he had enough playing tricks to coast within a trick of game and one trick is not too much to expect from a partner. He bid four hearts.

West was in the same spot as his counterpart on Hand No. 29. But he had a few more points and he too was entitled to hope that his partner held something. He bid five clubs. North, with seven diamonds, jumped in and bid five diamonds. East prayed for the house to catch on fire. But he did like diamonds.

South rebid hearts and West went to six clubs. By this time North believed silence was golden. He might have doubled, and chances are that Babe still would have bid six hearts. Had North doubled and South passed, the double would have been most unsuccessful.

Babe bid six hearts on the theory that he couldn't lose much, and now West doubled. Then West chose the unfortunate lead of the ace of diamonds. Babe trumped the ace, dropped West's singleton king of hearts, then he went to dummy's six of hearts by playing a smaller heart. He discarded his spade losers on the diamonds and made an overtrick.

It is no problem to be aggressive if you have good cards. In that case you only have to worry about getting into the right contract. Show your strength and your partner will respond and from his responses you are usually able to deduce which suit is the best. (We say usually. We all get in bad contracts on occasion.)

Under limit raises we pointed out that the jump bid puts your hand in a certain point range. In a sense each bid you make places certain limits on the maximum and minimum strength of your hand. Early bids have a wide spread of limits, succeeding bids progressively diminish these limits.

Certain bids demand further action by partner. There are two classes: one-round forces and game forces.

The following bids are one-round forces:

Any *response* in a new suit.
Any reverse bid by the responder.
Any bid of a new suit by the opening bidder *after the responder makes a two over one response.*

Here are bids that force one's partner to continue bidding at least until game is reached:

The opening bid of two of a suit.
Any jump in a new suit by the opening bidder or his partner (the jump shift).
Any immediate jump response of two no-trump.
Any bid of a new suit by responder after he has first responded with a new suit at the two level.

It should be noted that here, as in the case of the takeout double, an intervening bid by the other side does not require partner to bid, since the opponent has provided the bidder an opportunity for another bid. If either you or your partner doubles an opponent's bid after previously making a game force, the double may be left for penalty.

A reverse bid is made with a moderately strong hand. It is a bid of a second suit that will require your partner to go to a higher level if he wishes to support your first bid.

For example, you open the bidding with one club, your partner responds one heart, and you make a two-diamond call. If your partner wishes to support clubs, he must bid three. The natural sequence of bids would be one diamond by you, one heart by your partner, two clubs by you. In that case, partner could support at the two level if he preferred diamonds.

Hand No. 31 is an example of a reverse bid.

South has 18 points in high cards and some distribution values. He opens his five-card heart suit; North responds two clubs showing at least 11 points, enough to warrant game. South now bids his spades. North has minimum support in hearts and three small spades, but he also has a stopper in the unnamed suit and

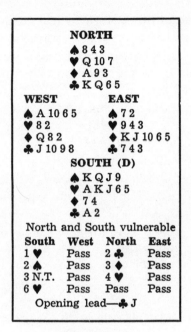

NORTH
♠ 8 4 3
♥ Q 10 7
♦ A 9 3
♣ K Q 6 5

WEST
♠ A 10 6 5
♥ 8 2
♦ Q 8 2
♣ J 10 9 8

EAST
♠ 7 2
♥ 9 4 3
♦ K J 10 6 5
♣ 7 4 3

SOUTH (D)
♠ K Q J 9
♥ A K J 6 5
♦ 7 4
♣ A 2

North and South vulnerable

South	West	North	East
1 ♥	Pass	2 ♣	Pass
2 ♠	Pass	3 ♦	Pass
3 N.T.	Pass	4 ♥	Pass
6 ♥	Pass	Pass	Pass

Opening lead—♣ J

Hand No. 31

a square (4-3-3-3) hand. His obvious bid is either no-trump or diamonds (which will not be taken as a suit bid, but as showing control of the suit). Because of the reverse bid by South and because a slam may be possible, North moves cautiously and bids the diamonds. When South bids three no-trump, North shows his heart support and South goes to six.

In the actual play South won the club lead in his hand, drew trumps with three leads ending in dummy, led a spade, rose with the king. West took his ace and then South squeezed him in the black suits and made the slam.

West might have broken up the squeeze by ducking spades twice. And East might have doubled the diamond bid, in which case West would have opened a diamond and spoiled the black-suit squeeze.

At this point, some reader is going to point out that the slam can be made with a diamond opening. However, this can only be done if you see all the cards. It involves the declarer running off all five trumps before starting to work on the spades. West would have to discard a diamond on the third trump lead and his last diamond on the fourth trump. The fifth trump would force a discard of a black card from West. A club discard would make all four of declarer's club tricks good. A spade discard would permit the declarer to make three spade tricks.

And, of course, we should point out that if East held the ace of spades, South would go down several tricks.

An opening bid of two in a suit shows a very powerful hand and is forcing to game. The minimum requirements are:

> At least 24 points, of which a minimum of 15 are in high cards, and an unbalanced distribution, such as a void suit, a singleton or two doubletons.

With 27 or more high-card points, you should make the two bid without hesitation. However, don't make the mistake of opening all powerful hands with two of a suit. Hands of balanced distribution with 21 to 26 points should be opened with two or three no-trump. Many other strong hands should be opened with a bid of one.

The responses show the strength in partner's hand. With from none to 6 points, bid two no-trump, showing your weakness, unless you have good support for your partner's major suit. If that is the case, bid four in his suit as a sign-off.

With 7 or more points, make a positive response by raising partner, showing a good suit of your own, or bidding three no-trump. Do not count distribution points in your hand unless you can support your partner's suit. High-card strength will be valuable, but distribution may be worthless in this kind of hand.

Hand No. 32 is an illustration of what distribution can do to you. South has a hand that would be opened at two by anyone.

This hand, sent to us by a lady from North Burnaby, British Columbia, was accompanied by the comment: "It looked as if

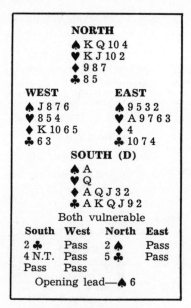

NORTH
♠ K Q 10 4
♥ K J 10 2
♦ 9 8 7
♣ 8 5

WEST
♠ J 8 7 6
♥ 8 5 4
♦ K 10 6 5
♣ 6 3

EAST
♠ 9 5 3 2
♥ A 9 7 6 3
♦ 4
♣ 10 7 4

SOUTH (D)
♠ A
♥ Q
♦ A Q J 3 2
♣ A K Q J 9 2

Both vulnerable

South	West	North	East
2 ♣	Pass	2 ♠	Pass
4 N.T.	Pass	5 ♣	Pass
Pass	Pass		

Opening lead—♠ 6

Hand No. 32

we had enough points for a small slam but we couldn't even make five clubs. Where did we go wrong?"

The error was in dealing North all those nice cards and giving South no way to use them. Any expert pair in the world who picked up those cards in the North and South hands would work their way beyond three no-trump — which my correspondent points out could be made — probably reaching six clubs or six diamonds.

Since you can see all the cards, you know that there is no defense against five clubs and, unless a heart is opened by the defense, no defense against six clubs. With the spade opening, South would draw trumps, lay down the ace of diamonds, lead the queen of hearts and overtake with dummy's king. If East takes his ace, he will have to lead a spade or a heart and South will discard four diamonds on the major-suit cards in the dummy.

Assume a heart opening and spade return. South plays two

rounds of trumps and the ace of diamonds. Then he would throw East into the lead by playing the deuce of trumps. East will have two tricks, but the rest belongs to South.

When you have spades, you can be not only aggressive, you can be a bully. Frequently your opponents will have a spade suit and use it to crowd the bidding until you get too high to make your contract. Or perhaps they will sacrifice and take a set of two or even three tricks to prevent you from scoring the points you might get for making a game or a slam.

Look at the West holding in Hand No. 33. It was rubber bridge and North was the late Charles Lockett of St. Louis, South was Oswald Jacoby, and West was the great expert Mr. Nameless.

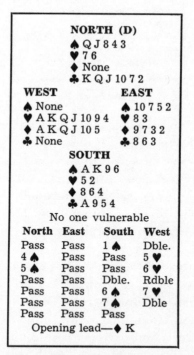

```
                NORTH (D)
                ♠ Q J 8 4 3
                ♥ 7 6
                ♦ None
                ♣ K Q J 10 7 2
WEST                        EAST
♠ None                      ♠ 10 7 5 2
♥ A K Q J 10 9 4            ♥ 8 3
♦ A K Q J 10 5             ♦ 9 7 3 2
♣ None                      ♣ 8 6 3
                SOUTH
                ♠ A K 9 6
                ♥ 5 2
                ♦ 8 6 4
                ♣ A 9 5 4
           No one vulnerable
```

North	East	South	West
Pass	Pass	1 ♠	Dble.
4 ♠	Pass	Pass	5 ♥
5 ♠	Pass	Pass	6 ♥
Pass	Pass	Dble.	Rdble
Pass	Pass	6 ♠	7 ♥
Pass	Pass	7 ♠	Dble
Pass	Pass	Pass	

Opening lead—♦ K

Hand No. 33

There was a grand slam in the West hand all by itself, but

there was one drawback. West held the red suits and Jacoby had opened a spade ahead of him. West believed that an immediate bid of seven would induce North and South to bid a defensive seven spades. Therefore West approached the slam cautiously by the bidding shown.

He made a takeout double and North jumped to four spades. West bid five hearts and North went to five spades. West bid six hearts, and Jacoby fell into the trap and doubled. West redoubled and Jacoby decided that West had 12 red cards. He ran out to six spades.

West tried seven hearts and Jacoby revised his thinking. West had 13 red cards. So Jacoby bid seven spades.

West could not go on, of course, and he doubled. Had West led a heart, the contract would have been defeated, but he led a diamond. Jacoby trumped with the eight of spades in dummy and led the three of spades and finessed the six. He ruffed a second diamond high, led the spade four and finessed the nine. He ruffed his last diamond, returned to his hand with the ace of clubs, drew trumps and discarded two hearts on the long clubs.

A spade suit is quite an advantage in the bidding.

In Hand No. 34, South showed power by means of a jump shift. You will recall that we pointed out that a hand could jump shift with 18 or more points, with at least 11 points in high cards.

This hand was made by play that should explain why experts are experts. The answer is that, as a matter of course, experts make plays that ordinary players would overlook.

The hand was played by Jan (Mrs. Tobias) Stone, one of the nation's best women players, in a rubber bridge game at the Cavendish Club in New York City. It shows faultless technique.

Jan opened one spade with a hand containing 20 high-card points. Her partner responded one no-trump. This was a bit of a stretch, viewed from the standpoint of book bidding, but it kept the bidding open for one round in the event partner had a good hand, which she did. Jan made a jump-shift to three hearts,

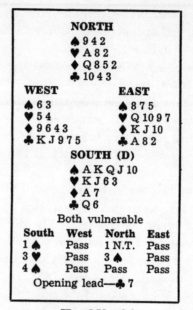

Hand No. 34

showing her power and forcing North to keep bidding until game was reached. When North responded three spades, South bid four.

Clubs were opened and continued. Jan ruffed the third club and played her ace of trumps. Then she led a low diamond and played the queen from dummy. East took his king and returned the suit to Jan's ace.

Most players would draw trumps at this point, then go after the hearts. The finesse would work, if South went to dummy with the ace and led a low heart through East's queen. But if East did not discard a heart when trumps were played, South would lose a trick in the end.

Jan did not draw trumps. She played one round of trumps, then led to dummy's ace of hearts and finessed through the queen. She played her king of hearts and trumped her fourth heart with dummy's nine, to make the contract.

Her refusal to draw the last trump gave her an extra chance

for her contract and risked nothing. If hearts had broken 3-3 she would have pulled that last trump. If West had held that last trump he would have made it by ruffing a high heart, but Jan would have been able to ruff her last heart with the trump she had retained in dummy and been set the same one trick she would have had to go down anyway.

6

Specialized Responses

IN tournament play, no-trump has an advantage over other suits. It takes only nine tricks to make a no-trump game, whereas major suits require ten and minor suits eleven.

But no-trump is risky unless you have a fistful of high cards and have each suit guarded satisfactorily. Sometimes it is better to explore major-suit possibilities. Very often a hand that will take only nine no-trump tricks will take ten in a suit and the extra points are worth going after in a match-point game.

Some specialized responses to an opening no-trump have been developed. Two of them are the Stayman two-club convention and the Jacoby transfer. You don't have to adopt these conventions to be a good player, but if you learn how to use them you will find them great aids.

The Stayman convention is a two-club response to an opening bid of one no-trump, and it is a forcing bid. In the Jacoby variation, the form we recommend as the most effective, the two-club response asks the opener to rebid as follows:

Two spades with four or more spades.
Two hearts with four or more hearts and less than four spades.
Two diamonds with any other holding.

In the Jacoby variation immediate three-club and three-diamond responses are weak, nonforcing bids. All other responses are normal.

After the original bidder does what his partner asks, it is up to the responder to rebid. He responds as follows:

With 8 points or less, he passes or bids two in a higher ranking suit.

With 9 or 10 points, he invites game by bidding two no-trump or by raising a two-spade or two-heart bid to three.

With 11 to 15 points, he bids a game in partner's major suit or in no-trump or jumps to three or four of his own major suit if he has one which is *more than* four cards in length.

With 16 or 17 points, he starts exploring slam possibilities with a bid of three diamonds or clubs, or by jumping to three spades over three hearts. This strength may be bid beyond game if partner's next bid is encouraging.

With 18 points or more, he bids slam immediately or forces with intention of eventually getting to slam.

The no-trump bidder will pass if responder has bid a game or two of a major suit. This is the same action that would be taken if Stayman were not being used.

If the responder has invited game by a bid of two no-trump or a raise in the suit he has bid, the original bidder will pass when he has a minimum no-trump hand, and go to game if he has above the minimum. He must decide whether to bid the game in no-trump or in the major suit. Partner has only 9 or 10 points, remember. A no-trump game usually requires 26 points, although with a solid suit and good stoppers it may be made on fewer points.

The opener *must* rebid if the responder has made a jump or has bid three in a minor suit.

Sam Stayman, who invented the Stayman convention with his partner, George Rapee, recommends a no-trump opening with the South hand shown in Hand No. 35.

Normally the no-trump hand is one with 4-3-3-3, 4-4-3-2, or 5-3-3-2 distribution, but the fact that the two doubletons in the

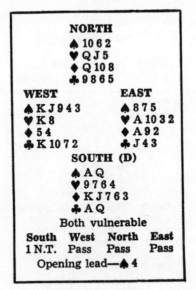

NORTH
♠ 10 6 2
♥ Q J 5
♦ Q 10 8
♣ 9 8 6 5

WEST
♠ K J 9 4 3
♥ K 8
♦ 5 4
♣ K 10 7 2

EAST
♠ 8 7 5
♥ A 10 3 2
♦ A 9 2
♣ J 4 3

SOUTH (D)
♠ A Q
♥ 9 7 6 4
♦ K J 7 6 3
♣ A Q

Both vulnerable

South	West	North	East
1 N.T.	Pass	Pass	Pass

Opening lead—♠ 4

Hand No. 35

South hand are so strong compensates in this case for the 5-4-2-2 distribution.

If South opens one no-trump, he will play the hand there. If West leads a spade, as he is quite likely to do in no-trump, South will have no trouble. He can establish his diamond suit with one lead, and with another trick in spades and the ace of clubs he is sure of his contract at least.

Now let's see what happens if South opens one diamond. West may overcall with one spade, whereupon he will eventually wind up with the contract at some number of spades. The hand will make three or four, depending on a lot of things.

If West passes, North may bid a no-trump, over South's one diamond. South may raise to two no-trump and is very likely to go down. If South passes, West may reopen with two spades. Should everyone pass, East may lead a spade, whereupon North will be set at his one no-trump contract.

Hand No. 36 shows Stayman at work.

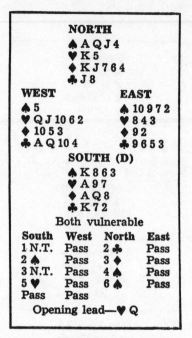

NORTH
♠ A Q J 4
♥ K 5
♦ K J 7 6 4
♣ J 8

WEST
♠ 5
♥ Q J 10 6 2
♦ 10 5 3
♣ A Q 10 4

EAST
♠ 10 9 7 2
♥ 8 4 3
♦ 9 2
♣ 9 6 5 3

SOUTH (D)
♠ K 8 6 3
♥ A 9 7
♦ A Q 8
♣ K 7 2

Both vulnerable

South	West	North	East
1 N.T.	Pass	2 ♣	Pass
2 ♠	Pass	3 ♦	Pass
3 N.T.	Pass	4 ♠	Pass
5 ♥	Pass	6 ♠	Pass
Pass	Pass		

Opening lead—♥ Q

Hand No. 36

Once again South opens with one no-trump. This time we can find no argument with the distribution. North has good spades and bids two clubs to ask South to show a four-card major. South bids two spades. Had South bid two hearts, North would have settled for game in no-trump.

Now North bids three diamonds, the all-purpose bid to show his strength, and South bids three no-trump because he has only 16 points and his partner has not *guaranteed* more than 11 points. (The North hand has the maximum of the 11- to 15-point range, but South cannot count on the maximum.)

North bids four spades, which is saying that he could have bid four over two, but he is interested in a slam and has strength in diamonds.

Now South takes another close look at his hand. He has first- or second-round control in every suit and North has diamonds and strong spades. He bids five hearts, and North goes to six spades.

After a heart opening, which South wins in dummy, he leads out the ace and queen of spades, learning the bad news about trumps. Then he takes the jack of spades, leads to his heart ace and trumps the third heart in dummy, returns to his hand with the ace of diamonds, picks up East's last trump and runs the rest of the diamonds. He concedes the final trick, the ace of clubs, but the slam is home.

Once you have mastered Stayman, you are ready to add the Jacoby transfer to your convention portfolio. We will call the convention JTB to simplify matters.

In the JTB you use the two-club response as we have explained it. Our variation of the Stayman convention is standard procedure in JTB.

Other parts of our transfer may sound complicated, but it is widely used and we are continually asked to illustrate it in our columns. When the Cleveland *Press* began using the Jacoby column, bridge editor Ben Creel said: "Let's start off with a week of JTB." So the obliging chaps at Newspaper Enterprise Association dug up a week's supply of JTB columns to give Cleveland readers their baptism.

In JTB the artificial responses are:

Two clubs is the Jacoby variation of Stayman.

Two diamonds is a transfer bid, showing at least five hearts and demands a two-heart rebid by opener.

Two hearts is also a transfer bid, showing at least five spades and demands a two-spade rebid by opener.

Two spades is highly artificial and will not come up often. It shows *both* minor suits and is forcing to game.

The other two-level responses are only one-round forces and may be made with anything from 0-25 points. The responder's second bid will clarify the picture.

Before we go further, we would like to repeat that our opening no-trump range is 15 to 17 points in high cards. This is in full accord with modern expert practice. If you want to use 16 to 18 no-trumps, we have no quarrel with it, but if you play 15 to 18, 14 to 16, or 11 to 14, you may be hurting yourself.

Jump responses to three or four in a major are made with normal holdings, but they should be made only when you want to be the declarer. Jumps to three clubs or three diamonds show weak hands. (There is no point in trying to get to a minor-suit game with a balanced hand.)

After an opening no-trump bid, if the second hand overcalls or doubles (says anything except *pass*), the transfer at the two-level is out entirely. You may move it to the four level, so that four diamonds becomes a transfer to hearts and four hearts a transfer to spades, but make sure your partner won't forget it. Two-level transfers are easy to remember, four-level transfers are not.

But if everything goes normally, if your response has been two clubs, carry on as you would under Stayman. If your response is two diamonds or two hearts, your partner will rebid two of your suit as you asked, whereupon your action depends on your holding. If you hold:

7 points or less, sign off by passing.

8 or 9 points, invite game by going to three in your suit or bidding two no-trump to give your partner a choice of passing, bidding three in your suit, three no-trump or four in your suit.

10 to 14 points, jump to game in your suit or bid three no-trump to give your partner a choice between the suit and no-trump. In either case he will be the declarer. If you have a two-suit hand, this is the time you should name your second suit. This is a force to game.

15 or more points, investigate slam possibilities. The advantage of the JTB is that it allows the no-trump bidder to remain as declarer, even though the hand is played in a suit. In other

words, the strength is concealed, as are the weaknesses.

When you use the JTB, you should make the two-diamond or two-heart transfer bid in preference to the two-club Stayman when you have one or more five-card (or longer) major suits and no four-card major. Use the Stayman two-club bid when you have four cards in one or both majors.

When you have bad club or diamond hands, jump right to three in your suit. Partner will pass. If you have a good minor, raise no-trump. It is easier to make nine tricks than eleven. With a very good minor-suit hand — both minors — respond two spades, a forcing bid. Otherwise respond two clubs and continue with three of your minor. Either of these bidding sequences should suggest slam possibilities.

In Hand No. 37, North's two-heart response was JTB. North had practically nothing excepting six spades headed by a king and, as you can see by looking at the hands, no-trump is very unsafe. South bid two spades and North's pass showed no interest in game.

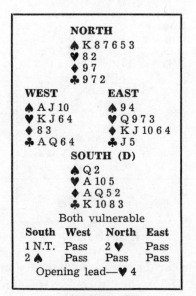

NORTH
♠ K 8 7 6 5 3
♥ 8 2
♦ 9 7
♣ 9 7 2

WEST
♠ A J 10
♥ K J 6 4
♦ 8 3
♣ A Q 6 4

EAST
♠ 9 4
♥ Q 9 7 3
♦ K J 10 6 4
♣ J 5

SOUTH (D)
♠ Q 2
♥ A 10 5
♦ A Q 5 2
♣ K 10 8 3

Both vulnerable

South	West	North	East
1 N.T.	Pass	2 ♥	Pass
2 ♠	Pass	Pass	Pass

Opening lead—♥ 4

Hand No. 37

At two spades, South won the opening heart and led the queen of trumps. Eventually he had to lose two trumps, one heart and two clubs, but he made his contract.

Hand No. 38 shows how JTB works with a fair hand. South opens a no-trump. North has seven points at no-trump. There is a chance, of course, that the long spades may develop some tricks, but if spades are trumps the North hand will be worth a great deal more. So North, using JTB, responds two hearts, South bids two spades and North goes to game.

West opened the queen of hearts, and South took his ace and led his king, in order to discard one of dummy's clubs before starting on trumps. He went on to make his contract, losing one trick in each suit except hearts.

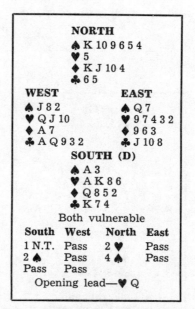

NORTH
♠ K 10 9 6 5 4
♥ 5
♦ K J 10 4
♣ 6 5

WEST
♠ J 8 2
♥ Q J 10
♦ A 7
♣ A Q 9 3 2

EAST
♠ Q 7
♥ 9 7 4 3 2
♦ 9 6 3
♣ J 10 8

SOUTH (D)
♠ A 3
♥ A K 8 6
♦ Q 8 5 2
♣ K 7 4

Both vulnerable

South	West	North	East
1 N.T.	Pass	2 ♥	Pass
2 ♠	Pass	4 ♠	Pass
Pass	Pass		

Opening lead—♥ Q

Hand No. 38

Had North been the declarer at four spades, as he might have been without the JTB at his disposal, East would very probably lead from the jack, ten, eight of clubs, giving his side two club tricks at the start and there would still have been a diamond and a trump trick to lose later. Down one.

In the course of a motor trip through the West a few years ago, Mr. and Mrs. Jacoby, Senior, played in a duplicate game in Laramie, Wyoming, where they picked up a hand (No. 39) that is a fine illustration of the JTB.

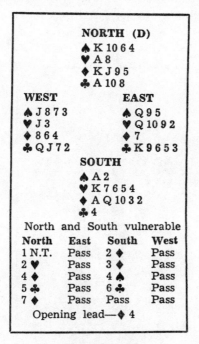

NORTH (D)
♠ K 10 6 4
♥ A 8
♦ K J 9 5
♣ A 10 8

WEST
♠ J 8 7 3
♥ J 3
♦ 8 6 4
♣ Q J 7 2

EAST
♠ Q 9 5
♥ Q 10 9 2
♦ 7
♣ K 9 6 5 3

SOUTH
♠ A 2
♥ K 7 6 5 4
♦ A Q 10 3 2
♣ 4

North and South vulnerable

North	East	South	West
1 N.T.	Pass	2 ♦	Pass
2 ♥	Pass	3 ♦	Pass
4 ♦	Pass	4 ♠	Pass
5 ♣	Pass	6 ♣	Pass
7 ♦	Pass	Pass	Pass

Opening lead—♦ 4

Hand No. 39

Mrs. Jacoby, sitting South, gave a JTB response of two diamonds to Ozzie's opening one no-trump. He dutifully responded two hearts, and she bid three diamonds, which showed diamonds as well as hearts and was forcing to game.

Ozzie liked diamonds better than hearts, and showed this by raising to four diamonds. Mr. Jacoby's four-spade bid showed the ace of spades and slam interest, so Ozzie bid five clubs to show that ace. Mrs. Jacoby's six-club call showed second-round club control and suggested a grand slam, which Ozzie proceeded to bid.

The play was very satisfactory. Mrs. Jacoby drew two rounds of trumps, cashed dummy's ace of hearts and her king, ruffed a heart, returned to her hand with the ace of spades, ruffed another heart, took dummy's ace of clubs, ruffed a club, pulled the remaining trump and took the final trick with her last heart.

Hand No. 40 shows another case in which four of a major suit makes, where three no-trump would fail.

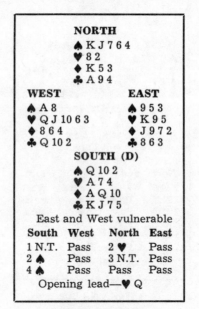

NORTH
♠ K J 7 6 4
♥ 8 2
♦ K 5 3
♣ A 9 4

WEST
♠ A 8
♥ Q J 10 6 3
♦ 8 6 4
♣ Q 10 2

EAST
♠ 9 5 3
♥ K 9 5
♦ J 9 7 2
♣ 8 6 3

SOUTH (D)
♠ Q 10 2
♥ A 7 4
♦ A Q 10
♣ K J 7 5

East and West vulnerable

South	West	North	East
1 N.T.	Pass	2 ♥	Pass
2 ♠	Pass	3 N.T.	Pass
4 ♠	Pass	Pass	Pass

Opening lead—♥ Q

Hand No. 40

North's two-heart response was JTB and after South responded, North jumped to three no-trump. In the JTB system, this shows just about the actual North hand, five spades, 10 to 14 high-card points and a no-trump distribution (5-3-3-2). South had a choice between playing three no-trump or four spades.

South had a square hand (4-3-3-3 distribution) with stoppers in all suits, and his first thought was to pass. But he looked long and hard at that lone heart stopper and realized his partner might have the same weakness, which is not unusual. Four spades would be a much safer spot.

The decision was wise. At four spades he lost one heart, one spade and one club. Had he passed three no-trump, a heart lead — which was the logical and best lead for West — would eventually set up four heart tricks before South could knock out the ace of spades, and South would have gone down one.

Of course JTB has no monopoly on successful bidding. North would have made four spades just as easily as South and lots of pairs would have arrived at four spades with North as declarer by using almost any system of responses.

But there are other hands where it will work in your favor. The point is, JTB helps you get to the best contract; no other convention can do more.

7

Convention City

A FOREST of conventions has grown around the game of contract bridge. Not one would have been developed unless it had some advantages, but it is reasonable to believe that all have certain disadvantages. The problem is to choose those that have the greater weight on the side of advantage. As long as bridge remains a game of logic, deduction and mathematical probabilities, we can't play without conventions. They are to a bridge player what clues are to a detective.

In our own slam bidding we use both the Blackwood four no-trump and the Gerber four-club conventions to ask for aces. In general Gerber is used as an adjunct to cover times when we want to use four no-trump as a strong bid in no-trump. In the Gerber convention, four diamonds over four clubs shows no aces or four aces; four hearts, one; four spades, two; and four no-trump, three.

In a tournament not very long ago Jacoby Sr. sat North and John Gerber sat South, and out of deference to the inventor of the convention, they were playing Gerber all the way. Hand No. 41 was a spot where the convention proved very useful.

Johnny might well have opened with a forcing two bid, but no one is ever passed out at one club (or seldom anyhow) and Johnny made his bid. When Ozzie jumped to two spades, Johnny was mildly surprised and delighted to find an ideal opportunity to use his convention. He bid four clubs. The four-spade response showed two aces and Gerber's four no-trump was a demand for kings. Jacoby bid five diamonds, showing one.

This made it possible for Johnny to count twelve top tricks and he bid seven as a very slight gamble. It seemed likely that North would have a queen or so extra for his initial jump-shift. (A jump shift shows at least 18 points with at least 11 high-card points.)

West opened the ten of diamonds and Jacoby put the queen and jack on the table first. At this point, Johnny said: "Show me no more!"

He spread his hand. He didn't need to see the rest because he knew from the bidding that his partner would hold two aces and a king and he had nine sure tricks in his hand. He had at least fourteen tricks if he needed them.

Of course the grand slam could have been bid in any system. At least it should have been, but the game was a team of four

---

Hand No. 41

NORTH
♠ A K J 10 8 6 5
♥ A 10 9 7
♦ Q J
♣ None

WEST
♠ Q 4
♥ Q 8 4 2
♦ 10 9 8 7
♣ 8 5 2

EAST
♠ 9 7 3
♥ K J 6 5
♦ 6 3 2
♣ 7 6 4

SOUTH (D)
♠ 2
♥ 3
♦ A K 5 4
♣ A K Q J 10 9 3

North and South vulnerable

South	West	North	East
1 ♣	Pass	2 ♠	Pass
4 ♣	Pass	4 ♠	Pass
4 N.T.	Pass	5 ♦	Pass
7 N.T.	Pass	Pass	Pass

Opening lead—♦ 10

Hand No. 42

NORTH
♠ K Q J 8 7 6 5 4 2
♥ A K
♦ 4
♣ 4

WEST
♠ 10
♥ J 10 9
♦ K J 8 7 3
♣ Q 9 7 3

EAST
♠ 9
♥ 8 6 4 3
♦ 10 9 5 2
♣ K J 6 5

SOUTH (D)
♠ A 3
♥ Q 7 5 2
♦ A Q 6
♣ A 10 8 2

No one vulnerable

South	West	North	East
1 N.T.	Pass	4 ♣	Pass
4 ♠	Pass	7 N.T.	Pass
Pass	Pass		

Opening lead—♥ J

and the opponents playing North and South stopped at six.

North and South in Hand No. 42 were two experts playing in a catch-as-catch-can rubber bridge game. But they were old-fashioned experts who did not put much faith in the Gerber convention.

Nevertheless, when South opened one no-trump, North decided he had a perfect hand to ask for aces the Gerber way. Expert North then could sign off at four spades or bid six after his partner responded, as the occasion demanded.

South read the four-club bid as Gerber and responded four spades. Fortunately for North and South's peace of mind, expert North was not fully acquainted with Gerber. In Blackwood, he knew that spades showed three aces, and without thinking he read the Gerber response as the same. As you can see, South had made the same mistake. So the double error canceled out. North counted thirteen tricks and bid seven no-trump.

The lesson to be drawn from this is: when playing Gerber, don't give Blackwood responses.

Harold S. (Mike) Vanderbilt, who invented contract bridge in 1927, also created the first bidding system, the Vanderbilt club. Mike Vanderbilt and Ozzie Jacoby won a national title using the convention, but Ozzie felt that one lost a trifle more than he gained when he gave up a normal club bid to use it artificially. The Jacobys still feel the same way, but Mike has added some new gadgets that should be of interest.

Under the Vanderbilt convention, after the opener bids a club, which shows at least 16 high-card points, one diamond denies holding (a) two aces; (b) one ace, one king and one queen; or (c) two kings and two queens. But it is forcing one round.

Any other response is forcing to game. A jump bid shows a solid suit of at least six cards. A further jump shows a solid suit of seven cards and an outside king, or a suit of eight cards.

Mike feels that aces and kings are so important in slam bidding that he counts ace-king points as well as high-card points.

When Hand No. 43 was played in a New Jersey regional, the standard bidding was usually one club by South, one spade by

North, and after some South players felt a slam might be made, they pushed to five spades, which went down under two defense aces and a heart ruff.

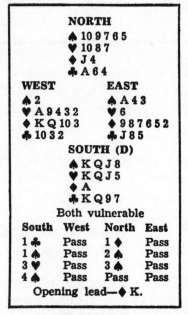

NORTH
♠ 10 9 7 6 5
♥ 10 8 7
♦ J 4
♣ A 6 4

WEST
♠ 2
♥ A 9 4 3 2
♦ K Q 10 3
♣ 10 3 2

EAST
♠ A 4 3
♥ 6
♦ 9 8 7 6 5 2
♣ J 8 5

SOUTH (D)
♠ K Q J 8
♥ K Q J 5
♦ A
♣ K Q 9 7

Both vulnerable

South	West	North	East
1 ♣	Pass	1 ♦	Pass
1 ♠	Pass	2 ♠	Pass
3 ♥	Pass	3 ♠	Pass
4 ♠	Pass	Pass	Pass

Opening lead—♦ K.

Hand No. 43

But it was bid as shown with the Vanderbilt club. The diamond response positively denied two aces, so South stopped at four.

In Hand No. 44, North jumped to three diamonds after South's opening Vanderbilt club, to show a solid suit. South's three-heart bid was a waiting measure and North's second jump to five diamonds was showing either an eight-card suit or a seven-carder with an outside king. It also denied an outside ace, because North would have cue-bid had he had one in addition to his solid suit.

South's five no-trump was a request for kings similar to Blackwood. South already knew his side had four aces, and when

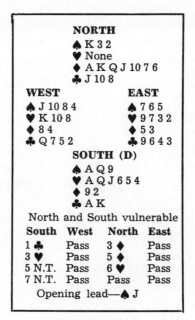

NORTH
♠ K 3 2
♥ None
♦ A K Q J 10 7 6
♣ J 10 8

WEST
♠ J 10 8 4
♥ K 10 8
♦ 8 4
♣ Q 7 5 2

EAST
♠ 7 6 5
♥ 9 7 3 2
♦ 5 3
♣ 9 6 4 3

SOUTH (D)
♠ A Q 9
♥ A Q J 6 5 4
♦ 9 2
♣ A K

North and South vulnerable

South	West	North	East
1 ♣	Pass	3 ♦	Pass
3 ♥	Pass	5 ♦	Pass
5 N.T.	Pass	6 ♥	Pass
7 N.T.	Pass	Pass	Pass

Opening lead—♠ J

Hand No. 44

North indicated two kings, South could count thirteen tricks —
seven diamonds, two clubs, at least three hearts or spades and
the other ace. South bid seven no-trump.

The forcing bid of two in a suit, discussed in Chapter 5, is an
integral part of standard bidding, but almost all experts use the
weak-two bid. At the 1965 world championship team trials, 35
of 36 pairs used this convention.

If you use it, you will have to abandon the bid of two in a
suit as forcing to game. However, under this convention, the
artificial bid of two clubs serves this purpose and is made on a
hand that would call for a standard forcing-to-game opening bid.
Two bids in the other three suits are weak bids, showing a good
six-card suit and a hand a trifle under the normal opening level
in high-card strength.

This is a slightly dangerous maneuver and, like all conventions, has disadvantages, but the experts think the bad points

are outweighed by the advantages. At any rate, you should be familiar with it, because someone will use it on you.

All experts do not use the bid the same way, but the American Contract Bridge League has fixed the limits as a minimum of 6 points and a maximum of 12 high-card points. In a tournament, a player who makes a weak-two call when his hand is outside these limits is penalized.

When the Jacobys use the weak two, our rules are rather strict. We must have a *good* six-card suit. Among the advantages of the weak two is that it gives you a chance to tell your partner what to lead if the opponents take the bid. Otherwise, with your weak hand you would be shut out of the bidding. But there is no point in telling your partner to lead a suit unless you have real strength in it.

We also vary our point count with vulnerability. We always try to have more than the minimum 6 points, and less than the maximum of 12 in honor count. And we do not open a weak two when we are void in a suit or have a four-card major-suit holding in addition to our six-carder.

After you have made your opening weak two, your partner has several alternatives, depending on his strength. He knows you are weak but have a good suit. If he sees that there is obviously no game in the hand, he will pass. A two no-trump response is forcing, the raise is an invitation to go on bidding, and the bid of a new suit is a message to play it there. Complicated responses are used by some players, but we have found these simple responses best.

After the two no-trump response, the original bidder sometimes has trouble making his reply descriptive of his hand. He will rebid his suit to show a minimum two hand, and another suit to show a fairly strong hand, within the range of 6 to 12 points, of course.

Hand No. 45 shows how a weak two produces a favorable result. None of the players here has a proper opening bid, but South has an excellent weak-two-heart bid with 9 high-card points and a good suit.

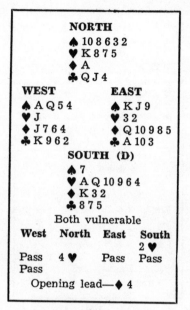

NORTH
♠ 10 8 6 3 2
♥ K 8 7 5
♦ A
♣ Q J 4

WEST
♠ A Q 5 4
♥ J
♦ J 7 6 4
♣ K 9 6 2

EAST
♠ K J 9
♥ 3 2
♦ Q 10 9 8 5
♣ A 10 3

SOUTH (D)
♠ 7
♥ A Q 10 9 6 4
♦ K 3 2
♣ 8 7 5

Both vulnerable

West	North	East	South
			2 ♥
Pass	4 ♥	Pass	Pass
Pass			

Opening lead—♦ 4

Hand No. 45

North does not know how good his partner's hand is, but he has excellent support for hearts, a singleton ace and there may be a club trick there as well. Spades are long, but since his partner has a six-card heart suit, there is likely to be a shortage of spades in South.

North's conclusion is that there is no reason to be scientific — if a game is there, they'll make it. If not, they won't be hurt badly. He bids four hearts.

A possible disadvantage of the weak-two is that it may make a pair miss a slam that would be reached if the weak-two bidder passed in the beginning.

North would open one diamond in third seat and jump to four spades after a one-spade response by South. South would try Blackwood and go right to six spades after North showed him two aces.

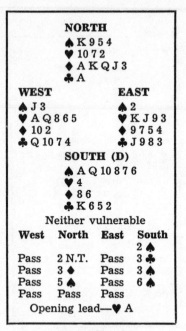

NORTH
♠ K 9 5 4
♥ 10 7 2
♦ A K Q J 3
♣ A

WEST
♠ J 3
♥ A Q 8 6 5
♦ 10 2
♣ Q 10 7 4

EAST
♠ 2
♥ K J 9 3
♦ 9 7 5 4
♣ J 9 8 3

SOUTH (D)
♠ A Q 10 8 7 6
♥ 4
♦ 8 6
♣ K 6 5 2

Neither vulnerable

West	North	East	South
			2 ♠
Pass	2 N.T.	Pass	3 ♣
Pass	3 ♦	Pass	3 ♠
Pass	5 ♠	Pass	6 ♠
Pass	Pass	Pass	

Opening lead—♥ A

Hand No. 46

The weak-two opening gives North a real problem. He surely has enough for game but slam is another problem.

The bidding in the box shows how a skillful pair handles this problem. North starts by making his only forcing response — two no-trump. South rebids to show a good opening two bid plus something in clubs and North's three-diamond bid is a further force after his two no-trump response. South's three-spade call shows nothing extra, but at this point North can make a key bid. He jumps to five spades. This bid says that everything is fine with spades, diamonds and clubs, but that North is worried about his heart losers. South has a singleton heart and goes on to six cheerfully.

As we pointed out, the weak-two bid is not perfect. Hand No. 47 displays a conspicuous failure of the convention.

West had a sound weak-two bid in spades and North had a

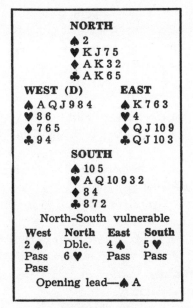

NORTH
♠ 2
♥ K J 7 5
♦ A K 3 2
♣ A K 6 5

WEST (D)
♠ A Q J 9 8 4
♥ 8 6
♦ 7 6 5
♣ 9 4

EAST
♠ K 7 6 3
♥ 4
♦ Q J 10 9
♣ Q J 10 3

SOUTH
♠ 10 5
♥ A Q 10 9 3 2
♦ 8 4
♣ 8 7 2

North–South vulnerable

West	North	East	South
2 ♠	Dble.	4 ♠	5 ♥
Pass	6 ♥	Pass	Pass
Pass			

Opening lead—♠ A

Hand No. 47

perfect hand for a takeout double, with strength in all suits except spades. East saw his own hand would not be effective against hearts, and he attempted to shut out South by a bid of four spades.

With a six-card heart suit, South would not be shut out and bid five hearts. West said pass, as he should have done. When a weak two is made, the bidder doesn't plan to bid past game.

North had to decide just how good his partner's five-heart bid was. East had crowded the bidding, but South's bid was free and North had strong outside support as well as four hearts headed by the king-jack. He bid a risky six.

When dummy went down, it appeared that South had not a chance in the world to make his bid, but he did so by a complicated squeeze.

West led his spade ace and shifted to a trump, which South won in his hand. He ruffed his last spade in dummy, then led trump four times. He discarded two clubs in dummy.

Dummy now had the ace-king of clubs and four diamonds to the ace-king. East also had to discard down to six cards and was squeezed in diamonds and clubs. Actually he held his diamonds to keep South from setting up a long-suit trick in that suit. Now South cashed dummy's ace and king of clubs, and ace and king of diamonds, and ruffed the third diamond in his hand to take the final trick with the eight of clubs.

The slam took expert play to bring home, but without the impetus of a weak two and the jump to game by East, it is doubtful if it would have been bid by North and South.

Thirty years ago the psychic bid and the name of Oswald Jacoby were almost synonymous. Ozzie did not invent the bid, but he certainly used it.

Then Ozzie gave it up. There were several reasons for this, such as the fact that as a person grows older he gains in conservatism, but the one important reason was that it cost him more points than it gained.

Few psychics are used nowadays. True, they have been used and will be used in tournaments, but they continue to set records for futility.

Hand No. 48 is an example. West's one no-trump was a psychic bid, made in hopes of confusing the opponents, getting them in the wrong contract, or keeping them out of game. West did not have diamonds stopped, as the bid would indicate if it were not a psychic, and he had nothing that would help much in a no-trump contract. He also did not have the intestinal fortitude necessary for a person who makes psychic bids. Had he stood by his guns and fought it out at one no-trump he would have been down only six tricks for a mere 1,100 points.

He started to escape with a redouble, which was not fortitude but an SOS, asking East to get him out of this fix. East responded with two clubs, his only suit and not much of one at that. Whereupon North and South proceeded happily to six no-trump.

This was too much for East, who doubled. Fortunately no one redoubled, for the slam was a laydown and North and

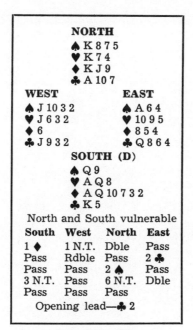

NORTH
♠ K 8 7 5
♥ K 7 4
♦ K J 9
♣ A 10 7

WEST
♠ J 10 3 2
♥ J 6 3 2
♦ 6
♣ J 9 3 2

EAST
♠ A 6 4
♥ 10 9 5
♦ 8 5 4
♣ Q 8 6 4

SOUTH (D)
♠ Q 9
♥ A Q 8
♦ A Q 10 7 3 2
♣ K 5

North and South vulnerable

South	West	North	East
1 ♦	1 N.T.	Dble	Pass
Pass	Rdble	Pass	2 ♣
Pass	Pass	2 ♠	Pass
3 N.T.	Pass	6 N.T.	Dble
Pass	Pass	Pass	

Opening lead—♣ 2

Hand No. 48

South scored 1,680 points. (An undoubled slam would have scored 1,440.)

The moral of this is that a psychic bid fools your partner as often as it fools your opponents.

Around 1935 Ely Culbertson designed the "asking bid." The bid was intended to ask partner about the holding in a specific suit. The convention lapsed into obscurity for a time, but recently Bob Nail and Bob Stucker of Houston began urging its use. Many of their asking bids are too complicated for general use, and possibly even for expert use. But one that appears to have merit is used after an opening of three hearts or spades.

This Stucker and Nail convention calls for a bid of four clubs to get a response from partner telling how good his trumps are. Four diamonds denies either the ace or the king; four hearts shows one of these two cards; four spades shows both; and four no-trump shows ace, king and queen. In all cases the

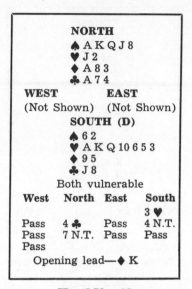

NORTH
♠ A K Q J 8
♥ J 2
♦ A 8 3
♣ A 7 4

WEST   **EAST**
(Not Shown)   (Not Shown)

SOUTH (D)
♠ 6 2
♥ A K Q 10 6 5 3
♦ 9 5
♣ J 8

Both vulnerable

West	North	East	South
			3 ♥
Pass	4 ♣	Pass	4 N.T.
Pass	7 N.T.	Pass	Pass
Pass			

Opening lead—♦ K

Hand No. 49

bidder is assumed to hold at least a seven-card suit for his pre-emptive bid. It is a move toward slam.

In Hand No. 49 only the bidder and responder's hands are shown. North doesn't care about anything in South's hand except his heart suit, and he responds four clubs after South's opening three-heart bid.

South bids four no-trump, showing ace, king and queen of hearts. North starts his mental computer working and adds seven hearts to his own six tricks and bids seven no-trump. He does not bid hearts because conceivably the opening lead might get ruffed at a heart contract.

You will note from the diagram that the asking bid solved all North's problems. Had South bid four diamonds to show he did not have the top hearts, North would have let the hand play at four hearts. North could have bid five hearts as an invitation to six had South rebid, to show he had one of the high cards, and he would have bid six hearts if South had rebid to four spades, to show both the ace and king but not the queen.

In Hand No. 50, look at the East hand. South has opened one no-trump and North has raised to three. You are East and all you can do is sit quietly and hope your partner will open a club. If only you had some way to tell him, without making an illegal signal, you could set the hand.

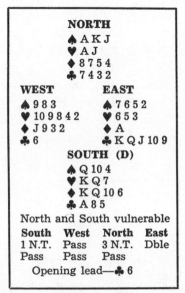

NORTH
♠ A K J
♥ A J
♦ 8 7 5 4
♣ 7 4 3 2

WEST
♠ 9 8 3
♥ 10 9 8 4 2
♦ J 9 3 2
♣ 6

EAST
♠ 7 6 5 2
♥ 6 5 3
♦ A
♣ K Q J 10 9

SOUTH (D)
♠ Q 10 4
♥ K Q 7
♦ K Q 10 6
♣ A 8 5

North and South vulnerable

South	West	North	East
1 N.T.	Pass	3 N.T.	Dble
Pass	Pass	Pass	

Opening lead—♣ 6

Hand No. 50

Dr. John Fisher of Dallas noticed that he was often in this position. Therefore, he reasoned, he would lose nothing if he reserved a double of three no-trump as a request to his partner to open a club. So he invented the Fisher double, which is a specific convention.

It is used when your partner is going to lead against three no-trump, reached without the bidding of any suit. It simply says: "Partner, lead a club."

This convention really falls into the gadget class. A person might adopt it and never have a chance to use it for several years, but when the chance comes and if you have explained the Fisher double to your partner, write it on your convention card so that your opponents can see it, and use it to advantage.

With the hand shown in No. 50, the club lead automatically beats the no-trump game. With any other lead, declarer will lead a diamond from dummy at some time and wind up making his contract.

In the pioneer days of contract bridge, the cue bid of an opponent's suit meant only one thing: first-round control. In modern expert usage it is used any time a player with a strong hand can find no better bid.

Sometimes it does show first-round control. Sometimes it is an invitation to no-trump. Still other times it is merely a general slam try to show second-round control.

In Hand No. 51, South holds only 12 points in high cards, but his hand is strong in distribution with a singleton and a doubleton.

```
                    NORTH
                    ♠ A 7
                    ♥ A K 6 2
                    ♦ 10 9 3
                    ♣ Q 10 7 3
    WEST                        EAST
    ♠ 10 5 2                    ♠ J 9 8 3
    ♥ Q 10 9                    ♥ J 8 5 3
    ♦ A K Q 8 6 4              ♦ J 7 2
    ♣ J                        ♣ 5 4
                    SOUTH (D)
                    ♠ K Q 6 4
                    ♥ 7 4
                    ♦ 5
                    ♣ A K 9 8 6 2
            Both vulnerable
    South   West    North   East
    1 ♣     1 ♦     1 ♥     Pass
    1 ♠     2 ♦     4 ♣     Pass
    4 ♦     Pass    6 ♣     Pass
    Pass    Pass
        Opening lead—♦ K
```

Hand No. 51

He opens with a club and West puts in an overall of one diamond. North bids a heart. South bids his four-card spade suit, which forces another bid from North. West again bids diamonds and North jumps to four clubs. After this jump, South has definite interest in a club slam. His problem is how to show his interest.

He can use Blackwood, and if North shows two aces, South can afford to bid six clubs. But if North bids five diamonds, to show only one ace, how will South get out of the hole with no exit? He would have to bid slam with two aces missing.

North probably does have two aces. His jump showed a strong hand, but he could have a sound four-club bid with only one ace. Four no-trump therefore is a bad bid.

The right bid is a cue bid of four diamonds, the suit that West bid and rebid. Possibly North will believe South is showing first-round control and jump to six with a single ace, but North has already bid pretty strongly and is unlikely to go slam crazy without two aces.

The four-diamond bid makes things easy for North. When he hears the call he considers going to seven, but he has bid a heart and jumped in clubs with only 13 high-card points, so he is content with six.

A convention known as the gambling no-trump had a vogue a few years ago. It called for an opening three no-trump with a solid suit, an honor or two outside, and a strong belief in predestination.

Hand No. 52 was played in a regional championship in St. Louis in 1952 with a couple of Californians holding the North-South cards.

Douglas Steen, sitting North, opened three no-trump and his partner, Bill Hanna, raised him to six.

A very unlucky expert, sitting East, doubled, whereupon Bill had to do some card reading. Obviously Doug's solid suit was clubs, and it was equally obvious that East had doubled with the ace, king and possibly the queen of hearts.

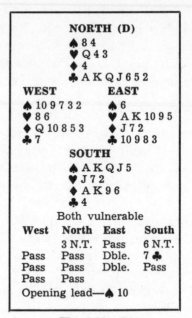

NORTH (D)
♠ 8 4
♥ Q 4 3
♦ 4
♣ A K Q J 6 5 2

WEST
♠ 10 9 7 3 2
♥ 8 6
♦ Q 10 8 5 3
♣ 7

EAST
♠ 6
♥ A K 10 9 5
♦ J 7 2
♣ 10 9 8 3

SOUTH
♠ A K Q J 5
♥ J 7 2
♦ A K 9 6
♣ 4

Both vulnerable

West	North	East	South
	3 N.T.	Pass	6 N.T.
Pass	Pass	Dble.	7 ♣
Pass	Pass	Dble.	Pass
Pass	Pass		

Opening lead—♠ 10

Hand No. 52

At six no-trump Bill would be down several tricks, but there might be hope in seven clubs. Bill gambled again and bid the grand slam in clubs.

Again the unlucky expert doubled, but not so cheerfully as he had voiced his previous call. It might be mentioned that the gambling no-trump was listed on the North-South convention cards, but the expert had not bothered to read the conventions they were using.

The expert had a right not to be cheerful because West had to decide which of three suits to lead and he guessed wrong. West opened the ten of spades and Bill drew trumps and claimed his grand slam.

8

Now Let's Play

IN the bidding of hands, bridge players usually are stating facts about their hands. (We except, of course, sacrifices, psychics, and errors.) Even an artificial bid is a fact. The facts are not conclusive, but usually are enough for the partner to draw sound conclusions about the suit and the contract the hand is capable of playing.

He deals with probabilities, which he deduces from the responses of his partner and the bidding, or lack thereof, by his opponents.

When it comes to playing the hand, the declarer sees all the cards his side holds. He must deal with probabilities if he is to know which of the two opposing hands contain cards that are a threat to his contract. The defense also sees 26 cards, but another 26 are divided between the defender's partner and the declarer.

About 40 years ago, Werner Heisenberg, a great physicist. formulated a theory about the unpredictability of electrons, which was called the "uncertainty principle." Although cards are not elections, they represent energy, or power, and are just as uncertain. But a skillful and watchful player can deduce what his opponents may hold.

The opening lead is just as important to the declarer as to the player who makes it, and there are certain fundamental book leads that players must be familiar with.

The person in the lead, who sits to the left of the declarer, will hold three kinds of suits: (a) long suits of four or more cards; (b) short suits of two or less; (c) three-card suits.

Against no-trump he will probably lead either the suit his partner bid, or from his long suit. It is always a good policy to lead partner's suit. Even if it does not work, your partner will maintain his friendship for you. But in no-trump, if your partner has not bid, you hope to establish the long cards of a suit of four or more.

In a suit contract, if you hold sufficient trumps to be able to use them before the declarer draws them, a short-suit lead may give you a trump trick. (Sometimes too it will help the declarer set up a long suit which he will use as a parking place for his losers after he has drawn trump!)

In general you open a three-card suit if your partner has bid it, or if there are good reasons not to lead any of your long or short suits.

The choice of a card is your next decision. The opening lead of fourth best of a long suit is a play that contract bridge inherited from its ancestors, auction bridge and whist. From this lead, your partner (and also your opponents) can tell how many cards of higher value are in the unseen hands. Simply subtract the face value of the card from eleven. For example, you lead a six. $11 - 6 = 5$. There are five cards higher than a six in the other three hands. Your partner looks in his hand and at the dummy and knows how many cards above the six are in declarer's hand.

Another lead, and sometimes a safer lead, is the top of a sequence that is solid or nearly so: K-Q-J, or K-Q-10. The exception is when you have a sequence headed by the ace and king. In that case lead the king. When you play (not lead) from a sequence, you play the bottom card, except when signaling strength, in which case you play the top. Generally, the play of a high card signifies strength; play of a low card, the lowest you have in the suit, signals weakness.

As we noted, leads in no-trump are different from suit leads.

Here you are trying to put the declarer at a disadvantage by making him lower his guard — that is, by making him play the stoppers in his suits, so that he will be defenseless against your strength. Therefore you save your aces for entries, and try to set up a lower card in some other long suit.

If you have a four-card suit headed by the king-queen, or queen-jack, you lead the highest card in a suit contract, but fourth best in no-trump. The exception is when your partner has bid the suit, in which case you lead the higher honor.

Bridge experts agree that if you have a three-card suit headed by two honors such as the king-queen or queen-jack, you lead the higher, but if you have three to a single honor, lead the lowest of the three. When it comes to a holding of three low cards, however, there is disagreement all over. We recommend you lead the lowest, and most experts agree, providing that your partner understands what you are doing.

When opening a doubleton, lead the top.

Commander Winfield Liggett said: "I care not who holds the nation's two bids, if I can make the killing opening lead."

In Hand No. 53, it looks as if South is a shoo-in for four hearts with a 23-point hand in high cards plus distribution values, even though North has only a jack and a doubleton to offer.

The bidding was normal with a two-heart opening, followed by North's negative reply, and an intermediate bid of diamonds by South, after which North shows his preference for hearts, then a game bid.

West has an "automatic lead" of the king of spades, the top of a sequence. It is the book lead and most players would make it, but West hesitates and remembers that South has shown a two-suiter and North, with a bad hand, has shown a preference for hearts. Suddenly it dawns on West that this is a time to disregard the book.

Instead, West leads the trump ace in order to destroy South's ruffing power, if possible. He follows this with a second trump,

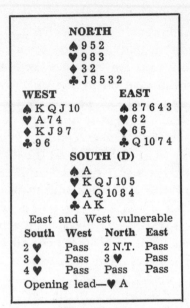

NORTH
♠ 9 5 2
♥ 9 8 3
♦ 3 2
♣ J 8 5 3 2

WEST
♠ K Q J 10
♥ A 7 4
♦ K J 9 7
♣ 9 6

EAST
♠ 8 7 6 4 3
♥ 6 2
♦ 6 5
♣ Q 10 7 4

SOUTH (D)
♠ A
♥ K Q J 10 5
♦ A Q 10 8 4
♣ A K

East and West vulnerable

South	West	North	East
2 ♥	Pass	2 N.T.	Pass
3 ♦	Pass	3 ♥	Pass
4 ♥	Pass	Pass	Pass

Opening lead—♥ A

Hand No. 53

which South takes with dummy's nine. South, of course, unblocked by dropping his ten of hearts on the first trick instead of playing the five.

Now South tries the diamond finesse, which loses, and West leads his third trump, which South must take in his hand. South cannot help losing two more diamond tricks to wind up down one.

Hand No. 54 shows another lead that was not according to the book, but which was made after careful consideration of the bidding. Ely Culbertson was in the South seat and Waldemar von Zedtwitz in the North. East was an expert, who will not be named. West was Oswald Jacoby.

From the bidding, it seemed likely that von Zedtwitz would be ready for either a diamond or a heart lead, which were not mentioned in the bidding. Ely had not encouraged spades after his partner's jump-shift, therefore he could not have much strength in it. But he would not have bid no-trump if he had

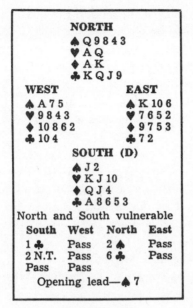

NORTH
♠ Q 9 8 4 3
♥ A Q
♦ A K
♣ K Q J 9

WEST
♠ A 7 5
♥ 9 8 4 3
♦ 10 8 6 2
♣ 10 4

EAST
♠ K 10 6
♥ 7 6 5 2
♦ 9 7 5 3
♣ 7 2

SOUTH (D)
♠ J 2
♥ K J 10
♦ Q J 4
♣ A 8 6 5 3

North and South vulnerable

South	West	North	East
1 ♣	Pass	2 ♠	Pass
2 N.T.	Pass	6 ♣	Pass
Pass	Pass		

Opening lead—♠ 7

Hand No. 54

had a singleton spade; therefore he must have at least two. Furthermore, Ely must have nearly a minimum hand, otherwise he would have found another rebid.

At this time, Jacoby had not seen the dummy, but he began to wonder about spades. If East held the queen of spades back of dummy's king, Ely would never read the lead and would play low from dummy. Two spade tricks would set, if Jacoby underled his ace.

Out popped the seven of spades. As soon as the dummy went down Jacoby regretted his action. His lead would not really have hurt if his partner had not held both the king and the ten. But the nine was played from dummy. East played the ten and Ely got a surprise trick with the jack and eleven expected tricks in the other suits.

Perhaps Jacoby's partner should have played his king instead of the ten, but it was a case where too much thinking helped the opponents make a slam.

As soon as the dummy is exposed, the declarer plans the play of the hand. There are four keys to the planning, which can be remembered by the word ARCH.

A is for ANALYZE the lead.
R is for REVIEW the bidding.
C is for COUNT your winners and losers.
H is for "HOW can the contract be made?"

In Hand No. 55, South analyzed the lead and reviewed the bidding to conclude that West held both missing aces. This left South with the possibility of losing a club and two spade tricks, providing East led spades or South had to play them himself. Therefore, counting winners and losers, the contract could be set.

But how to make the contract?

Two lines of play suggested themselves. West might have led

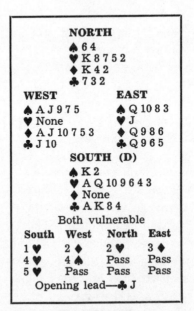

```
                    NORTH
                    ♠ 6 4
                    ♥ K 8 7 5 2
                    ♦ K 4 2
                    ♣ 7 3 2
        WEST                    EAST
        ♠ A J 9 7 5             ♠ Q 10 8 3
        ♥ None                 ♥ J
        ♦ A J 10 7 5 3         ♦ Q 9 8 6
        ♣ J 10                 ♣ Q 9 6 5
                    SOUTH (D)
                    ♠ K 2
                    ♥ A Q 10 9 6 4 3
                    ♦ None
                    ♣ A K 8 4
                 Both vulnerable
      South    West    North    East
      1 ♥      2 ♦     2 ♥      3 ♦
      4 ♥      4 ♠     Pass     Pass
      5 ♥      Pass    Pass     Pass
         Opening lead—♣ J
```

Hand No. 55

the jack of clubs as the top of a jack-ten-nine sequence. South might let the jack hold and later he could discard a losing spade from dummy on his own fourth club.

South's review of the bidding indicated that West had a long diamond suit, possibly six in view of South's own shortage, but the spade bid showed probably five spades. If the cards were 6-5, West would only hold two clubs and the lead was the top of a doubleton.

The alternate play made it necessary for South to take the first club, lead a heart to dummy's king and then play clubs from dummy. He would duck so that West would have to lead, whereupon his only choice would be a diamond or a spade, and West would lose only one spade. (A diamond would set up dummy's king for a spade discard.)

However, Sally Johnson of Westport, Connecticut, who sat East, had also used the word ARCH, with the H standing for HOW can this hand be set? She assumed that West had led from a doubleton club, and she also assumed that, with the club lead, South would duck or finesse against her queen. She played her queen, and South had to take it, dropping West's ten and making Sally's nine the setting trick.

A great many players would flounder in Hand No. 56 by failing to go through the four steps represented by the cue word ARCH.

West opens the king of diamonds and continues with the queen and nine. East takes the third diamond with the ace and leads the ten of clubs. West's queen forces dummy's ace and South plays two rounds of trumps. West discards the jack of diamonds on the second trump.

Up to this point, South hasn't had to do much thinking. But if he is to make this contract, he must find a way to avoid losing a heart trick. Some players would lead a heart to the dummy's ace and finesse the jack on the way back. West would take with his queen and the hand would go down the drain.

But players who review the bidding would realize that West

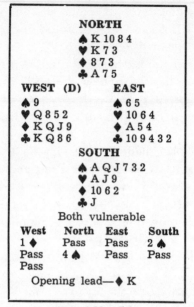

NORTH
♠ K 10 8 4
♥ K 7 3
♦ 8 7 3
♣ A 7 5

WEST (D)
♠ 9
♥ Q 8 5 2
♦ K Q J 9
♣ K Q 8 6

EAST
♠ 6 5
♥ 10 6 4
♦ A 5 4
♣ 10 9 4 3 2

SOUTH
♠ A Q J 7 3 2
♥ A J 9
♦ 10 6 2
♣ J

Both vulnerable

West	North	East	South
1 ♦	Pass	Pass	2 ♠
Pass	4 ♠	Pass	Pass
Pass			

Opening lead—♦ K

Hand No. 56

would need the queen of hearts for his opening bid. East has played the ace of diamonds, and only 17 points could possibly be in the East and West hands. West would not be likely to open a minor suit with only 11 points. Besides, East would have responded if he had held a queen in addition to his ace.

An expert would figure out that if West held the queen of hearts and East the ten, he could make the hand. The odds would be against this being the case, but it would be the best chance to make the hand.

South therefore would lead the jack from his own hand. If West ducked, South would let it ride. If West covered, South would win with the king and finesse against East's ten.

If South had been the dealer in Hand No. 57 he probably would have reached four spades without any adverse bidding and he would have tried the heart finesse and gone down.

Fortunately, East was dealer and South reached four spades

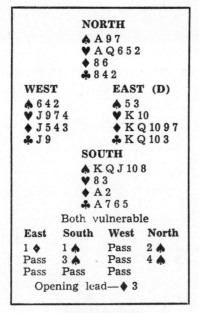

NORTH
♠ A 9 7
♥ A Q 6 5 2
♦ 8 6
♣ 8 4 2

WEST
♠ 6 4 2
♥ J 9 7 4
♦ J 5 4 3
♣ J 9

EAST (D)
♠ 5 3
♥ K 10
♦ K Q 10 9 7
♣ K Q 10 3

SOUTH
♠ K Q J 10 8
♥ 8 3
♦ A 2
♣ A 7 6 5

Both vulnerable

East	South	West	North
1 ♦	1 ♠	Pass	2 ♠
Pass	3 ♠	Pass	4 ♠
Pass	Pass	Pass	

Opening lead—♦ 3

Hand No. 57

anyhow, but East had made a diamond bid. The lead, of course, was a diamond from West to his partner's bid. South won the trick with his ace and decided that West probably led his fourth best from the jack.

A review of the bidding marked East with the king of hearts. South was sure the finesse would not work. He counted his tricks and decided that he would lose a diamond and two clubs, and, if he couldn't come up with something, he would lose a heart. How would he avoid it?

One way was to finesse and hope that the hearts would break 3-3 so he could set up two heart tricks in dummy, but there was a better way.

He assumed hearts would break 4-2, but he really didn't care if they broke 3-3 as long as East held the heart king.

He led the eight of hearts and let it ride. East won with the ten and cashed a diamond before he led the king of clubs. South won with the ace and led a heart to dummy's ace. East dropped the king and South ruffed a low heart in his hand and drew trumps. He stopped in dummy and discarded two clubs on his long hearts and conceded one club trick at the end.

When you try to locate your opponents' cards by reviewing the bidding, it is just as important to remember what has *not* been said as the things you hear. In other words, a pass may be just as informative as a bid, as in Hand No. 58.

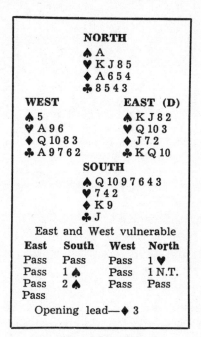

NORTH
♠ A
♥ K J 8 5
♦ A 6 5 4
♣ 8 5 4 3

WEST
♠ 5
♥ A 9 6
♦ Q 10 8 3
♣ A 9 7 6 2

EAST (D)
♠ K J 8 2
♥ Q 10 3
♦ J 7 2
♣ K Q 10

SOUTH
♠ Q 10 9 7 6 4 3
♥ 7 4 2
♦ K 9
♣ J

East and West vulnerable

East	South	West	North
Pass	Pass	Pass	1 ♥
Pass	1 ♠	Pass	1 N.T.
Pass	2 ♠	Pass	Pass
Pass			

Opening lead—♦ 3

Hand No. 58

South won the first trick in dummy because he needed the king of diamonds as an entry to his hand. He cashed dummy's ace of trumps, came to his hand with the king of diamonds and played the spade queen, hoping to smother the jack. But West played the seven of clubs and East was in with the king of spades.

East led the king of clubs and continued with the queen, which South ruffed. Then South led the ten of trumps and East took his jack and led another club. South again ruffed and extracted East's last trump.

South now had three hearts, one trump and a slight headache, which was caused by the fact that he had to lead a heart and guess whether to play dummy's king or jack.

A review of the bidding was like aspirin. There was no guess at all on the position of the ace of hearts. East had already played the king and jack of spades — valued at four high-card points — and the king and queen of clubs — five more points. If East had held the ace of hearts he would have had a total of 13 high-card points, enough to open the bidding. But East did not open his mouth during the bidding. With the jack of diamonds in the East hand, the total would be 14 points, which would certainly have caused East to bid. (A player *may* open with 13 points, but he *should* open with 14.)

South led a low heart and West played low. Certain that West held the ace of hearts and had ducked, South went right up with dummy's king and made his two-spade contract.

John Crawford, who became a tournament player at eighteen, and not so long ago announced his retirement from tournaments at the age of fifty, pulled Hand No. 59 out of thin air, after he let his opponent review the bidding.

It was a slam contract with Oswald Jacoby in the North seat and John sitting South in an all-expert rubber bridge game.

When Ozzie raised Johnny's two-heart bid to three, the slam idea began to formulate. Almost any bridge player sitting in Johnny's spot with a good 14-point hand across from a major-suit opening and support for the second major, which happened to be a six-carder, would think this way. But Johnny did not do what just any bridge player would do at this point, which would have been to use Blackwood.

Instead Johnny put in an unnecessary bid of four clubs. If you glance at the hands, you will see that the one lead Johnny wanted was a club lead to his ace-queen tenace. To bid clubs might stop that lead.

But Johnny knew his West opponent. When the slam was bid, West reviewed the bidding. At this point, we should point out that the defense can use the ARCH principle, too.

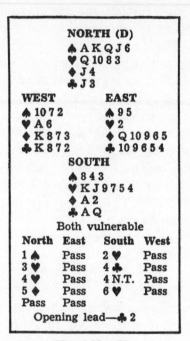

NORTH (D)
♠ A K Q J 6
♥ Q 10 8 3
♦ J 4
♣ J 3

WEST
♠ 10 7 2
♥ A 6
♦ K 8 7 3
♣ K 8 7 2

EAST
♠ 9 5
♥ 2
♦ Q 10 9 6 5
♣ 10 9 6 5 4

SOUTH
♠ 8 4 3
♥ K J 9 7 5 4
♦ A 2
♣ A Q

Both vulnerable

North	East	South	West
1 ♠	Pass	2 ♥	Pass
3 ♥	Pass	4 ♣	Pass
4 ♥	Pass	4 N.T.	Pass
5 ♦	Pass	6 ♥	Pass
Pass	Pass		

Opening lead—♣ 2

Hand No. 59

West's answer to why Johnny bid four clubs was that Johnny was trying to stop a club lead. West opened a club and the slam came home.

A diamond lead would have beat Johnny's slam, and West's hand offered little choice between clubs and diamonds. Of course West *might* have led clubs anyway, but there was a fifty-fifty chance he would lead diamonds.

The uncertainty principle is always ready to lead to the unexpected in bridge. The word ARCH tells the player how to win more times than he loses, but there is such a word as ARCHED, with the extra letters standing for EXCEPT DECEIVING bids.

One more Hand, No. 60, belongs in this chapter on first things to do. We have purposely left it to last because it illustrates that anything can happen and even a usually unsound play can be successful.

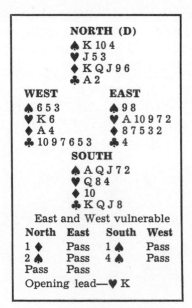

NORTH (D)
♠ K 10 4
♥ J 5 3
♦ K Q J 9 6
♣ A 2

WEST　　　**EAST**
♠ 6 5 3　　　♠ 9 8
♥ K 6　　　♥ A 10 9 7 2
♦ A 4　　　♦ 8 7 5 3 2
♣ 10 9 7 6 5 3　♣ 4

SOUTH
♠ A Q J 7 2
♥ Q 8 4
♦ 10
♣ K Q J 8

East and West vulnerable

North	East	South	West
1 ♦	Pass	1 ♠	Pass
2 ♠	Pass	4 ♠	Pass
Pass	Pass		

Opening lead—♥ K

Hand No. 60

Most of the time the way to win at bridge is to stick to the turnpike and let your opponents gallivant up and down the side roads, but an occasional trip into the boondocks may prove rewarding.

Now look closely at the West hand and review the bidding. Your opponents have reached spades on simple, straightforward bidding; obviously South expects to make his contract and has the material to justify that expectation. Then how can you beat the hand?

You see that trumps will break nicely for declarer and that you will make exactly one diamond trick. Then where will three more tricks come from? The best chance is in the heart suit. If your partner just happens to hold the ace of hearts and you open your king you should collect two heart tricks and a ruff. Of course, you may be putting your king's head on the chopping block, but you probably aren't giving away anything more than one extra trick if you lead it right into declarer's ace-queen.

So you lead out your king of hearts and enterprise is rewarded. The king holds; your partner's ace takes the second trick; you ruff the third heart and still have your ace of diamonds left.

9

Make the Contract

ONE of the basic principles of play in a suit contract is that the declarer should draw trumps as soon as he can do so with safety. He must first make sure that he has no need to ruff in the short hand. If he does, he should delay pulling trumps until he has taken care of it.

In Hand No. 61, South opens one spade. With 19 points in high cards he is too strong for a one no-trump bid and too weak for a bid of two no-trump. North has eight supporting points in spades, but it would not help as much in no-trump. North raises to two and the South hand is worth the jump to game.

West opens the king of hearts and South counts his winners and losers. He has two potential heart losers, a sure diamond loser and a sure club loser. But he can eliminate one heart loser by ruffing in dummy.

Therefore, South cannot draw trump right away. He must take the first trick with his ace and return hearts. When he gets in again he will ruff his third heart with the ten or king of trumps. The three would do just as well, but he can afford to use an honor and by doing so he eliminates the danger of an overtrump by East.

Then South draws trumps and either concedes a club or a diamond or plays out the hand, just in hope that a squeeze might develop or his opponents make a mistake.

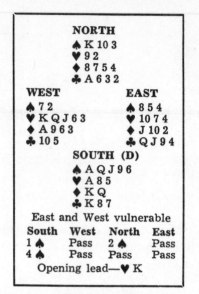

NORTH
♠ K 10 3
♥ 9 2
♦ 8 7 5 4
♣ A 6 3 2

WEST
♠ 7 2
♥ K Q J 6 3
♦ A 9 6 3
♣ 10 5

EAST
♠ 8 5 4
♥ 10 7 4
♦ J 10 2
♣ Q J 9 4

SOUTH (D)
♠ A Q J 9 6
♥ A 8 5
♦ K Q
♣ K 8 7

East and West vulnerable

South	West	North	East
1 ♠	Pass	2 ♠	Pass
4 ♠	Pass	Pass	Pass

Opening lead—♥ K

Hand No. 61

In this hand, the defense would be well aware of what South was trying to do. West might have led spades after taking South's heart return in order to shorten dummy's trump, but it would not have done West much good. South needed only one ruff in dummy to make his contract.

But Hand No. 62 shows where such a lead might be damaging. It also illustrates what is known as a "dummy reversal" play.

The hand was played in the National Intercollegiate Bridge Tournament and was prepared by Bill Root and Larry Rossler. The hands are first bid and then, irrespective of the actual bidding contract, are played at a directed final contract. The contestants are graded on both their bidding and play.

In this hand South is supposed to reach a four-heart contract and West is directed to open the ten of trumps. Without a trump lead, South would have one spade loser and two trump losers. But against that trump lead, South has two possible spade losers. His problem is to cause one of them to vanish.

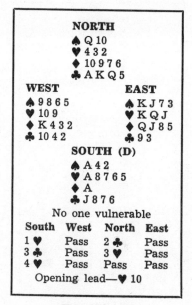

NORTH
♠ Q 10
♥ 4 3 2
♦ 10 9 7 6
♣ A K Q 5

WEST
♠ 9 8 6 5
♥ 10 9
♦ K 4 3 2
♣ 10 4 2

EAST
♠ K J 7 3
♥ K Q J
♦ Q J 8 5
♣ 9 3

SOUTH (D)
♠ A 4 2
♥ A 8 7 6 5
♦ A
♣ J 8 7 6

No one vulnerable

South	West	North	East
1 ♥	Pass	2 ♣	Pass
3 ♣	Pass	3 ♥	Pass
4 ♥	Pass	Pass	Pass

Opening lead—♥ 10

Hand No. 62

To make the dummy reversal, he ducks the first trump lead and wins the continuation. Then he cashes the ace of diamonds, enters dummy with a club, ruffs a diamond in his hand. He returns to dummy with a second club and ruffs another diamond with his next to last trump and leads a third club to dummy.

East can ruff this trick if he desires, but then he will have no trump left to lead and South will get his spade ruff. East's best play is to discard and South will play clubs again. East can ruff or discard and no matter what he does, South makes his contract.

Hand No. 63, is another example of a dummy reversal play. It was accomplished by Charlton Wallace, who has been bridge editor of the *Cincinnati Post and Times-Star* almost as many years as the elder half of Jacoby & Son has been playing tournament bridge. He sat South in this game.

Charlton's jump to six hearts in a rubber bridge game was a

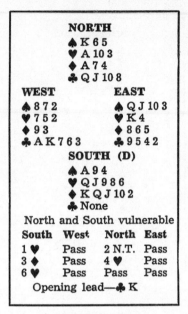

NORTH
♠ K 6 5
♥ A 10 3
♦ A 7 4
♣ Q J 10 8

WEST
♠ 8 7 2
♥ 7 5 2
♦ 9 3
♣ A K 7 6 3

EAST
♠ Q J 10 3
♥ K 4
♦ 8 6 5
♣ 9 5 4 2

SOUTH (D)
♠ A 9 4
♥ Q J 9 8 6
♦ K Q J 10 2
♣ None

North and South vulnerable

South	West	North	East
1 ♥	Pass	2 N.T.	Pass
3 ♦	Pass	4 ♥	Pass
6 ♥	Pass	Pass	Pass

Opening lead—♣ K

Hand No. 63

shot in the dark, but he had a good play for the slam if the trump finesse would work. It did not, and that is what makes it a good story.

He took the finesse after he ruffed the opening club lead, and after East produced his king of trumps, Charlton had a spade trick to eat. He could have afforded to lose the spade if the finesse had worked.

He won the trump return in dummy and ruffed a second club. Then he entered dummy with the king of spades and ruffed a third club. This left Charlton with no trumps, which was what he wanted. He went to dummy with the ace of diamonds and led dummy's last trump. On this he discarded his losing spade and dropped West's last trump.

Charlton refused to take credit for the play, pointing out that similar hands could be found in his own writings. It was a book play, but a mighty good one. Anyone can write 'em up, but it takes an expert to make them.

In Hand No. 63, a finesse failed, as it will half the time. The finesse is a much-abused tactic, but it is also frequently used since sometimes there is no alternative.

Good poker players think they are unlucky when they don't win all the time. Good bridge players expect to be lucky because they try not to give bad luck a chance to hurt them if they can avoid it.

In Hand No. 64, anyone would want to be in three no-trump with the North-South cards and almost everyone would bid to get there.

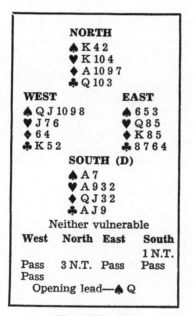

NORTH
♠ K 4 2
♥ K 10 4
♦ A 10 9 7
♣ Q 10 3

WEST
♠ Q J 10 9 8
♥ J 7 6
♦ 6 4
♣ K 5 2

EAST
♠ 6 5 3
♥ Q 8 5
♦ K 8 5
♣ 8 7 6 4

SOUTH (D)
♠ A 7
♥ A 9 3 2
♦ Q J 3 2
♣ A J 9

Neither vulnerable

West	North	East	South
			1 N.T.
Pass	3 N.T.	Pass	Pass
Pass			

Opening lead—♠ Q

Hand No. 64

A good player would bring home the contract, while most of the others would go down because they would lose both the club and diamond finesses. The point is that the good player would lose the finesses and still make the contract.

Most players understand about ducking when they are afraid of a suit that is opened. In Hand No. 64, South would duck the first spade lead and win the second.

A careless player would follow this by taking the diamond

finesse, which would lose. Another spade lead would knock out dummy's king and South would go down after the loss of the club finesse and the playing of West's two good spades.

An expert South would see that he could afford to lose both finesses if he took them in the right order. He would lead a heart to dummy's king at trick three and try the club finesse first. It would lose and West would set up his spades. But now South would come to his hand with a club and try the diamond finesse. It would lose, but East would not have a spade to lead to his partner.

An expert takes a finesse as a matter of course and his chief concern is when to refuse one.

Hand No. 65 illustrates such an occasion. South is in a comfortable six-spade contract after his partner has opened the bidding with one diamond.

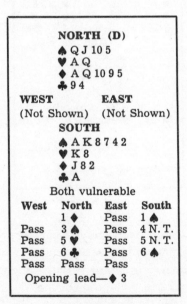

	NORTH (D)		
	♠ Q J 10 5		
	♥ A Q		
	♦ A Q 10 9 5		
	♣ 9 4		

WEST	EAST
(Not Shown)	(Not Shown)

	SOUTH
	♠ A K 8 7 4 2
	♥ K 8
	♦ J 8 2
	♣ A

Both vulnerable

West	North	East	South
	1 ♦	Pass	1 ♠
Pass	3 ♠	Pass	4 N. T.
Pass	5 ♥	Pass	5 N. T.
Pass	6 ♣	Pass	6 ♠
Pass	Pass	Pass	

Opening lead—♦ 3

Hand No. 65

for South. He would win in his own hand and draw trumps. Then he would lead the diamond jack, intending to play low from dummy.

If West has the king of diamonds, the finesse will succeed. Put the king in the East hand, and it will not. In either case South will make his contract. An extra trick will be his reward if the finesse works.

But West does the usual, and makes a killing lead of a diamond. There is danger if South finesses now. West might have opened a singleton diamond. If South lost the finesse, East would return his partner's lead and West would trump. South would go down one.

The ace of diamonds play guarantees the contract unless East is void in diamonds. This is a possibility, but a singleton lead is far more likely. South refuses the finesse.

The double finesse is one against two missing cards. In Hand No. 66, South misses the king and queen of spades. If he lays down the ace, he will lose two spade tricks and go down, unless one of those high cards is a singleton. If he leads from dummy and finesses the ten, planning to finesse the jack later, he will lose two spade tricks if West holds both honors.

The chance of West's holding both honors is such that South will win one of the two finesses three times out of four. But here, as you can see, West holds both honors, and the hand falls into the 25 percent group in which both finesses will fail. If South finesses twice, he will be set one trick.

Most South players who try a double finesse on a hand such as this will complain about their bad luck, but a South player who knows how to play will have no complaint.

There is no law compelling him to take the second finesse if the first one fails, and he can avoid the second finesse if he plays correctly.

He wins the opening lead and draws trump. Then he plays the three high clubs and dummy's remaining high diamond.

He leads the spade from dummy and puts the ten on the trick.

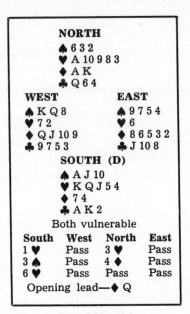

NORTH
♠ 6 3 2
♥ A 10 9 8 3
♦ A K
♣ Q 6 4

WEST
♠ K Q 8
♥ 7 2
♦ Q J 10 9
♣ 9 7 5 3

EAST
♠ 9 7 5 4
♥ 6
♦ 8 6 5 3 2
♣ J 10 8

SOUTH (D)
♠ A J 10
♥ K Q J 5 4
♦ 7 4
♣ A K 2

Both vulnerable

South	West	North	East
1 ♥	Pass	3 ♥	Pass
3 ♠	Pass	4 ♦	Pass
6 ♥	Pass	Pass	Pass

Opening lead—♦ Q

Hand No. 66

West takes the trick and that is all the finessing South has to do. If West returns a spade, South automatically takes his ace and jack of spades. If West leads a diamond, South ruffs in one hand and discards a losing spade in the other. The same thing happens to a club lead.

In most finessing situations you risk a trick in the hope of gaining one. But in some cases the finesse cannot lose. Hand No. 67 is an example.

West's one-spade overcall on this hand gave South a problem. A two-diamond rebid would be inadequate, as would one no-trump, and three diamonds or two hearts would distort his hand. A slight overbid of two no-trump was the best answer.

North went to three no-trump and West opened the queen of spades. South looked at the dummy and was delighted to see that his contract would make if he could bring home four diamond tricks.

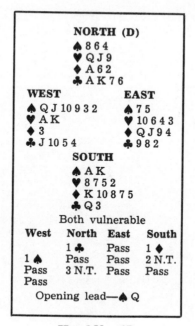

NORTH (D)
♠ 8 6 4
♥ Q J 9
♦ A 6 2
♣ A K 7 6

WEST
♠ Q J 10 9 3 2
♥ A K
♦ 3
♣ J 10 5 4

EAST
♠ 7 5
♥ 10 6 4 3
♦ Q J 9 4
♣ 9 8 2

SOUTH
♠ A K
♥ 8 7 5 2
♦ K 10 8 7 5
♣ Q 3

Both vulnerable

West	North	East	South
	1 ♣	Pass	1 ♦
1 ♠	Pass	Pass	2 N.T.
Pass	3 N.T.	Pass	Pass
Pass			

Opening lead—♠ Q

Hand No. 67

South was also one of those players who believed all suits should break nicely. After he won the opening trick he led a diamond to dummy's ace. He returned a diamond and went up with the king after East played the nine. Then he lost his smile. Why did everything happen to him? Eventually he went down two tricks.

This would not have happened had South taken an elementary precaution. He should have covered East's nine of diamonds with the ten. He might lose to West, had West held the queen or the jack, but his contract would have been safe. There was no way for South to avoid losing one diamond trick, which would not have set him, but playing the ten would have guaranteed that he would not lose two.

Hand No. 68 properly belongs in the chapter on the squeeze play, but we are putting it here to show that the finesse is not the answer to everything.

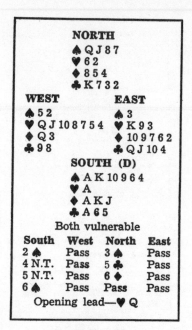

NORTH
♠ Q J 8 7
♥ 6 2
♦ 8 5 4
♣ K 7 3 2

WEST
♠ 5 2
♥ Q J 10 8 7 5 4
♦ Q 3
♣ 9 8

EAST
♠ 3
♥ K 9 3
♦ 10 9 7 6 2
♣ Q J 10 4

SOUTH (D)
♠ A K 10 9 6 4
♥ A
♦ A K J
♣ A 6 5

Both vulnerable

South	West	North	East
2 ♠	Pass	3 ♠	Pass
4 N.T.	Pass	5 ♣	Pass
5 N.T.	Pass	6 ♦	Pass
6 ♠	Pass	Pass	Pass

Opening lead—♥ Q

Hand No. 68

South opened with a forcing two-spade bid and North scraped the bottom of the barrel to find a positive response. South went into Blackwood and was delighted that he had stopped at six when he saw the dummy.

He had to lose a club and, unless clubs were kind enough to break 3-3, he would have to do something about his jack of diamonds. The normal play would be to finesse. You can see that the finesse is going to lose, but if South could just peek into an opponent's hand he would see that he could drop the diamond queen from the West hand by simply playing out his ace and king. One peek is sometimes worth more than a finesse. In this case, South was able to get the same information by simply watching his opponents' discards and going through a process known as "counting the hand."

He won the heart lead and played out a couple of trumps,

taking note of the fact that East discarded a diamond on the second trump. Then he led a club and allowed West to hold the trick with the eight.

West led a second heart, which South ruffed, and then South proceeded to lead out his last three trumps. East had to make three discards. One was a heart; the other two were diamonds. West also had to make three discards, but they were all hearts. Dummy's one discard was a low diamond.

Now South cashed his ace of diamonds and ace of clubs. Everyone followed. South led his last low club and West discarded a heart, while dummy's king won the trick. At this point everyone was down to two cards. Dummy held a low diamond and a low club. East held a low club and a mystery card that had to be either the last remaining heart or the queen or ten of diamonds, while West was marked with either two diamonds or a diamond and a heart.

South finally played the last diamond from dummy. East followed with the ten, but South was able to play his king of diamonds, drop West's queen and make his contract. He had located the queen of diamonds just as surely as if he had seen all the cards.

We are frequently asked: "What is the single most important bit of advice you would give an average player?" It is a tough question to answer, but there is one bit of advice that every beginner, average player and expert would do well to follow: When you are declarer, get into the habit of thinking about the whole hand before you play the first card from dummy.

This advice will also speed up your play. Take a look at Hand No. 69.

South played the deuce of hearts from dummy after West made his opening lead of the jack. Maybe he had heard the cliché, "Second hand low." Or perhaps he failed to stop a couple of seconds for thought.

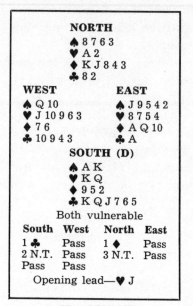

NORTH
♠ 8 7 6 3
♥ A 2
♦ K J 8 4 3
♣ 8 2

WEST
♠ Q 10
♥ J 10 9 6 3
♦ 7 6
♣ 10 9 4 3

EAST
♠ J 9 5 4 2
♥ 8 7 5 4
♦ A Q 10
♣ A

SOUTH (D)
♠ A K
♥ K Q
♦ 9 5 2
♣ K Q J 7 6 5

Both vulnerable

South	West	North	East
1 ♣	Pass	1 ♦	Pass
2 N.T.	Pass	3 N.T.	Pass
Pass	Pass		

Opening lead—♥ J

Hand No. 69

Now he was in his own hand. He took a moment or two to think and he realized that he had to attack the club suit. He led the king and East won with the ace.

East led a second heart and South was in dummy. East showed out when South led a second club. Now it was time for deep thought that should have been taken before the first play. But there was no way to make the hand. The best South could do was to continue clubs and let West get a second club trick, after which West cashed three hearts and led a diamond to his partner. South lost two diamonds for down three.

Had South stopped to think on the first play from dummy, he would have won the trick there and led a low club. East would have had to play his ace. Then all of South's remaining five clubs would have been winners, and two hearts and two spades would have made his contract of three no-trump. He would also have saved a lot of time, because he would have only stopped once to think.

We have shown that "second hand low" is not always a good rule, especially when applied to the declarer. "Third hand high" also has exceptions. However, third hand should play high unless there is a definite reason to play low. Hand No. 70 is an example.

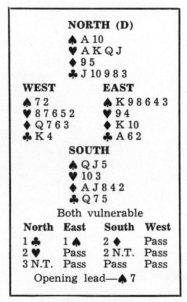

NORTH (D)
♠ A 10
♥ A K Q J
♦ 9 5
♣ J 10 9 8 3

WEST
♠ 7 2
♥ 8 7 6 5 2
♦ Q 7 6 3
♣ K 4

EAST
♠ K 9 8 6 4 3
♥ 9 4
♦ K 10
♣ A 6 2

SOUTH
♠ Q J 5
♥ 10 3
♦ A J 8 4 2
♣ Q 7 5

Both vulnerable

North	East	South	West
1 ♣	1 ♠	2 ♦	Pass
2 ♥	Pass	2 N.T.	Pass
3 N.T.	Pass	Pass	Pass

Opening lead—♠ 7

Hand No. 70

West opened the seven of spades against the three no-trump contract with South as declarer. South played the ten from dummy. Should East play his king?

It is a sure trick and by not playing the king, East may be throwing away his chances of making it good. But if East wants to beat three no-trump, he should play the nine of spades.

South will probably overtake dummy's ten with his jack and lead a club toward dummy. It will be up to West to play his king and lead another spade. He would have been surprised when East failed to cover dummy's ten of spades, but he will have noted the play of the nine to show strength instead of a low spade to show weakness.

This second spade lead will establish the rest of the spade suit for East, while he still holds the ace of clubs for a sure entry.

If East clatters up with the king of spades at trick one he can return the suit, but he can never get any more tricks in it because when West gets in with the king of clubs he won't have a spade to lead.

10

No-Trump Play

WE have discussed no-trump bidding and a few no-trump hands along the way, but this chapter will be devoted entirely to the play of no-trump hands. As in previous chapters, we will start with the simple hands and work to those more complex.

Hand No. 71 is a typical teacher's problem in which the declarer, South, must get his ninth trick for game. The solution is to capture two club tricks. Most of the time he will get those two tricks no matter how he plays the club suit, but there is only one line of play that will *guarantee* those two tricks.

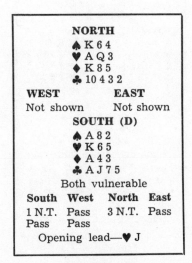

NORTH
♠ K 6 4
♥ A Q 3
♦ K 8 5
♣ 10 4 3 2

WEST   **EAST**
Not shown   Not shown

SOUTH (D)
♠ A 8 2
♥ K 6 5
♦ A 4 3
♣ A J 7 5

Both vulnerable

South	West	North	East
1 N.T.	Pass	3 N.T.	Pass
Pass	Pass		

Opening lead—♥ J

Hand No. 71

South must play his ace of clubs. If he drops an honor, his worries are over. If either opponent shows out, he will have no trouble. If East shows out, he will lead toward his dummy's ten, and if West shows out, he leads toward the jack in his own hand. Two such leads will knock out the king and queen of clubs, or give declarer his second club trick.

If both opponents follow, on the first lead, South plays another club toward dummy's ten. If West shows out, South plays the ten to force one of the honors and his jack will be an eventual trick. If West follows low, South plays dummy's ten and he is sure of an eventual trick because the only two clubs not accounted for are the king and queen.

In Hand No. 72, North and South were using the Jacoby version of Stayman, the purpose of which is to find a 4-4 major-suit fit. South's two-diamond rebid denied a four-card major.

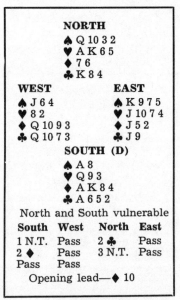

NORTH
♠ Q 10 3 2
♥ A K 6 5
♦ 7 6
♣ K 8 4

WEST
♠ J 6 4
♥ 8 2
♦ Q 10 9 3
♣ Q 10 7 3

EAST
♠ K 9 7 5
♥ J 10 7 4
♦ J 5 2
♣ J 9

SOUTH (D)
♠ A 8
♥ Q 9 3
♦ A K 8 4
♣ A 6 5 2

North and South vulnerable

South	West	North	East
1 N.T.	Pass	2 ♣	Pass
2 ♦	Pass	3 N.T.	Pass
Pass	Pass		

Opening lead—♦ 10

Hand No. 72

Twenty-six points is normal for a no-trump game, but in this case, South with 29 points, had his problems. He ducked the opening lead of the ten of diamonds, and won the continuation. Then he led his eight of spades and put in dummy's ten when West played low. East won with the king, a fortunate break, but that was the way South hoped things would happen.

East led his last diamond. At this point South could see nine tricks and since the game was duplicate he tried for an overtrick. He discarded a spade from dummy and led the deuce of clubs. He played dummy's eight and East won with the nine. (West had played low.)

This play would give him ten tricks if either hearts or clubs broke and besides it offered squeeze possibilities. But nothing worked. Nevertheless, South was satisfied with making his contract.

We have frequently mentioned ducking a trick, and in no-trump it is extremely important as a precaution against a long suit. For example, West leads from a suit long enough to set the contract if it is established. By ducking once or twice, you may exhaust the cards of this suit in the second opponent's hand so he cannot lead back the suit if he gets in the lead.

Hand No. 73 was another from the 1963 National Intercollegiate Bridge Tournament, sponsored by the Association of American Playing Card Manufacturers.

Some optimists might raise their partner's opening one no-trump to four with 15 high-card points and 4-3-3-3 distribution, but we play it as a very sound three no-trump bid. At best, there will be only a poor play for slam and at worst there might be trouble making four.

Either three or four no-trump was a par contract in the tournament and the problem was for South to make that tenth trick.

West was directed to open the king of diamonds, to lead a high diamond whenever possible and never to discard a club. These instructions are common sense, because the club jack is the only entry to the West hand outside the diamond suit.

South can see nine easy tricks; if clubs break, he will have his

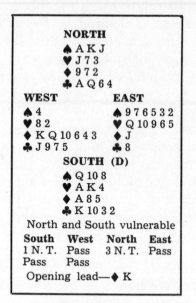

NORTH
♠ A K J
♥ J 7 3
♦ 9 7 2
♣ A Q 6 4

WEST
♠ 4
♥ 8 2
♦ K Q 10 6 4 3
♣ J 9 7 5

EAST
♠ 9 7 6 5 3 2
♥ Q 10 9 6 5
♦ J
♣ 8

SOUTH (D)
♠ Q 10 8
♥ A K 4
♦ A 8 5
♣ K 10 3 2

North and South vulnerable

South	West	North	East
1 N.T.	Pass	3 N.T.	Pass
Pass	Pass		

Opening lead—♦ K

Hand No. 73

tenth. But in a par contest as well as in actual play, one must allow for bad breaks.

South ducks the first trick. The queen of diamonds is played, and when East shows out, there is no longer any reason for South to duck. He plays his ace. Now he goes after the clubs, but when the ace and queen are played from dummy, East shows out in that suit also. Now South cashes three spades and two hearts. West has to discard two diamonds and South knows that he is left with two high diamonds and the jack-nine of clubs. It is a simple matter to throw West in with a diamond and force him to lead a club up to South's king-ten. This will give South his tenth trick.

Hand No. 74 shows when not to play second hand low.

If North had bid three no-trump instead of three hearts, the trouble with spades would not have materialized. But East had bid spades and North did not know that South held the king.

When West opened the eight of spades, South remembered

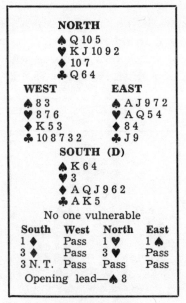

NORTH
♠ Q 10 5
♥ K J 10 9 2
♦ 10 7
♣ Q 6 4

WEST
♠ 8 3
♥ 8 7 6
♦ K 5 3
♣ 10 8 7 3 2

EAST
♠ A J 9 7 2
♥ A Q 5 4
♦ 8 4
♣ J 9

SOUTH (D)
♠ K 6 4
♥ 3
♦ A Q J 9 6 2
♣ A K 5

No one vulnerable

South	West	North	East
1 ♦	Pass	1 ♥	1 ♠
3 ♦	Pass	3 ♥	Pass
3 N.T.	Pass	Pass	Pass

Opening lead—♠ 8

Hand No. 74

the rule "Second hand low, unless there is a definite reason to play high." South does have a definite reason to play high.

East had bid a spade, West led the eight spot. Therefore, all of the higher spades were in the East hand. If South plays the five from dummy, East will play the nine. If South plays the ten, East will play the jack. In either case, South will have to win with his king and when West gets in he will lead a second spade, dummy's queen will be dead, and South will lose four spade tricks. He is also going to lose a trick to the ace of hearts, and if the diamond finesse doesn't work (which it won't), he will lose a diamond trick.

With a strong reason then, South plays the queen of spades from dummy. If East wins with the ace and leads back spades, South will let it ride to dummy's ten and will still have a spade stopper. If East ducks, South will take his diamond finesse immediately. It will lose, but a spade return will allow South to make four no-trump.

If West shifts to a heart, South will make three no-trump. But the queen of spades play at trick one assures his contract.

You know by now, if you have not already been aware, that no-trump contracts demand stoppers in all suits. Your opponents are certain to attack your weakness and you should have at least some kind of defense. Hand No. 75 is an example of this.

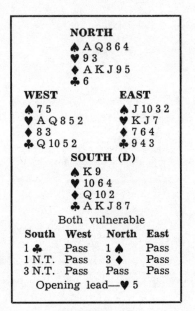

NORTH
♠ A Q 8 6 4
♥ 9 3
♦ A K J 9 5
♣ 6

WEST
♠ 7 5
♥ A Q 8 5 2
♦ 8 3
♣ Q 10 5 2

EAST
♠ J 10 3 2
♥ K J 7
♦ 7 6 4
♣ 9 4 3

SOUTH (D)
♠ K 9
♥ 10 6 4
♦ Q 10 2
♣ A K J 8 7

Both vulnerable

South	West	North	East
1 ♣	Pass	1 ♠	Pass
1 N.T.	Pass	3 ♦	Pass
3 N.T.	Pass	Pass	Pass

Opening lead—♥ 5

Hand No. 75

North could have made four spades on this hand by ruffing the third heart and playing three rounds of trumps. That would leave East with a good trump, but North would lead diamonds and clubs until East chose to ruff.

Five diamonds would also make. North would have to play the king and ace of spades and ruff a low spade with one of dummy's high trumps before drawing trumps, but if he selected this line of play he could bring home the contract.

But three no-trump did not make because the defense took five heart tricks before South could get in the lead. Naturally each partner of the North-South pair believed it was not his fault and that the other should have taken the contract somewhere else. The fault was South's. He bid no-trump over his partner's spade and three no-trump over his partner's three diamonds. After the second no-trump bid, North was entitled to credit his partner with at least one stopper in hearts.

South had a difficult bid over three diamonds, but that problem could have been solved by a three-spade call. North would not have gone to four without a five-card suit. South could also have properly bid four diamonds.

The reason an expert seems to play without problems is that he sees his problems coming and works out a solution in advance. He is therefore ready for them when they arrive.

In Hand No. 76, West was an expert and he made the normal lead of the jack of spades against South's seven no-trump.

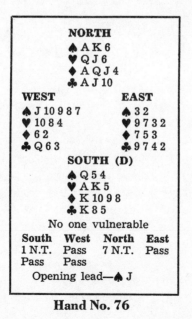

NORTH
♠ A K 6
♥ Q J 6
♦ A Q J 4
♣ A J 10

WEST
♠ J 10 9 8 7
♥ 10 8 4
♦ 6 2
♣ Q 6 3

EAST
♠ 3 2
♥ 9 7 3 2
♦ 7 5 3
♣ 9 7 4 2

SOUTH (D)
♠ Q 5 4
♥ A K 5
♦ K 10 9 8
♣ K 8 5

No one vulnerable

South	West	North	East
1 N.T.	Pass	7 N.T.	Pass
Pass	Pass		

Opening lead—♠ J

Hand No. 76

When the dummy hit the table, West added his 3 high-card points to dummy's 22; the total of 25 meant that 15 points were in South's hand and in his partner's hand. Since South had opened the bidding with one no-trump, which meant a minimum of 15 high-card points, it was apparent that East's hand was without a single face card.

Therefore South would have a minimum of 12 tricks off the top, three each in spades and hearts, four in diamonds and two in clubs. Should declarer have four hearts, he was certain of thirteen tricks. If declarer had four spades, then West's only chance to defeat the contract was to hang on to three of his remaining four spades, now that he had played the jack. Solving his problem in advance, West decided he would probably have to discard a club somewhere along the route.

The problem arose as expected. South cashed four diamonds and three hearts. West put a heart and a spade on the diamonds, but he was forced to throw a club on the third heart. Since all this had been anticipated, he discarded the three of clubs without a bit of worry.

Declarer cashed two more spades. East had to discard and he let a club go and now South knew that East had started with four clubs and West with three. It seemed likely that East would hold the queen of clubs and South finessed that way.

West made both his queen of clubs and the last spade to set the contract two tricks.

South could have tried the club finesse earlier and gone down only one, but when a grand slam is in the balance one or two doesn't make a great deal of difference.

In Chapter 13 we will discuss swindle plays at some length. Although Hand No. 77 might seem to be an example of such a play, it really is less a swindle than a case of bad bidding on the part of South.

Most North-South pairs would arrive at a four-heart contract, which could be made. In fact an overtrick is possible. Three no-trump looks just about as easy.

South would duck twice on spades and then he would later lose the heart finesse. East would lead back a diamond and, while

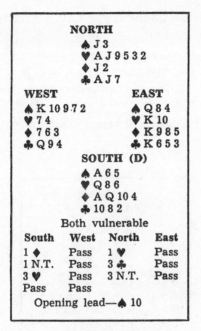

NORTH
♠ J 3
♥ A J 9 5 3 2
♦ J 2
♣ A J 7

WEST
♠ K 10 9 7 2
♥ 7 4
♦ 7 6 3
♣ Q 9 4

EAST
♠ Q 8 4
♥ K 10
♦ K 9 8 5
♣ K 6 5 3

SOUTH (D)
♠ A 6 5
♥ Q 8 6
♦ A Q 10 4
♣ 10 8 2

Both vulnerable

South	West	North	East
1 ♦	Pass	1 ♥	Pass
1 N.T.	Pass	3 ♣	Pass
3 ♥	Pass	3 N.T.	Pass
Pass	Pass		

Opening lead—♠ 10

Hand No. 77

South would have an uneasy moment finessing into the West hand, there would be no alternative and the finesse would work. He would run off the rest of the heart suit and eventually finesse diamonds again to make four no-trump.

Nevertheless, in a rubber bridge game, South managed to go down one trick at three no-trump.

The first few plays were as advertised; on the fourth play, South led the six of hearts and finessed dummy's jack. Not only did the finesse work, but East dropped the ten.

South decided that East had started with a singleton ten of hearts. If this were the case, South had to return to his hand for a second finesse. He led the jack of diamonds.

An East who could hold back the king of hearts from a king-ten doubleton could also play low on the jack of diamonds. South rose with the ace and led the queen of hearts.

He let it ride. Anybody would. East produced the king and

led a club. South ran off the rest of his hearts, but he had to give East the last two tricks.

Sometimes one card is very important, as can be seen in Hand No. 78, which diagrams a game in which Jim Jacoby and Dr. John Fisher of Dallas just missed making the international bridge team not long ago. They were so close in the last round that if Jim, sitting East, had held the king of spades they would have made the team.

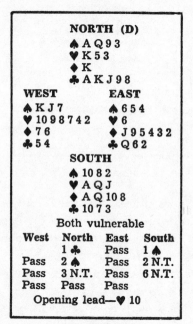

NORTH (D)
♠ A Q 9 3
♥ K 5 3
♦ K
♣ A K J 9 8

WEST
♠ K J 7
♥ 10 9 8 7 4 2
♦ 7 6
♣ 5 4

EAST
♠ 6 5 4
♥ 6
♦ J 9 5 4 3 2
♣ Q 6 2

SOUTH
♠ 10 8 2
♥ A Q J
♦ A Q 10 8
♣ 10 7 3

Both vulnerable

West	North	East	South
	1 ♣	Pass	1 ♠
Pass	2 ♠	Pass	2 N.T.
Pass	3 N.T.	Pass	6 N.T.
Pass	Pass	Pass	

Opening lead—♥ 10

Hand No. 78

Sam Stayman was South, playing a six no-trump contract, and John opened the ten of hearts. Stayman won in his hand and led a club to dummy's king. Then he led the king of diamonds and came back to his hand with another heart. He lost the club finesse to Jim.

Young Jacoby led a club right back and Sam ran off the rest of dummy's clubs and discarded two spades. Then he overtook dummy's king of hearts with his ace and cashed the ace and queen of diamonds. This left him with the tens of spades and diamonds and Jim was down to the jack of diamonds and the six of spades. John held the king and jack of spades.

Because Jim had shown out on the second heart and John on the third diamond, Sam had a perfect count of the hand and knew that the king of spades was an exactly even-money proposition.

Sam led his ten of spades and John played the jack. This didn't help Sam, because John would have played the jack irrespective of whether the other card was the king or the six.

Sam studied for five minutes, then called for the queen of spades from dummy.

Had Fisher and Young Jacoby set the contract they would have scored fourteen International Match Points, but instead they lost ten.

Hand No. 79 shows a play that goes back to around 1935 or 1936, and reflects a rather tricky problem. The question is: Can South make his normal three no-trump contract against perfect defense?

Declarer can count three club tricks, three diamond tricks, two hearts and a spade, provided he can get them all in.

As you study the hand you will see that one or maybe two duck plays are necessary. Thus, when spades are played, South must let East's queen hold the first trick in order to shut out West's long spades. If hearts are played, South must duck the second heart in order to shut out East's fourth heart.

A good average player can see all this. After a while he might be cajoled into betting that he could make the hand. At that point the trap would be sprung, because perfect defense will hold South to eight tricks.

The six of spades is opened and East's queen holds the trick. The five of spades is led back. West takes his ace and sets up his last two spades by playing a low card.

Doesn't South now go over to dummy and lead a diamond in

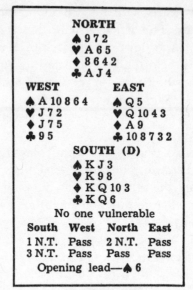

NORTH
♠ 9 7 2
♥ A 6 5
♦ 8 6 4 2
♣ A J 4

WEST
♠ A 10 8 6 4
♥ J 7 2
♦ J 7 5
♣ 9 5

EAST
♠ Q 5
♥ Q 10 4 3
♦ A 9
♣ 10 8 7 3 2

SOUTH (D)
♠ K J 3
♥ K 9 8
♦ K Q 10 3
♣ K Q 6

No one vulnerable

South	West	North	East
1 N.T.	Pass	2 N.T.	Pass
3 N.T.	Pass	Pass	Pass

Opening lead—♠ 6

Hand No. 79

order to establish three diamond tricks?

Not if East is worth his salt. East would discard his ace of diamonds on the third spade. (At least this is what he would do if he were looking at all the cards and, after all, this is a problem.)

Now the jack of diamonds becomes an entry to the West hand and South is set.

Over the past forty years, probably no bridge player has got himself into more trouble in the bidding than our old friend Walter Malowan, and in our opinion no one has successfully worked himself out of more bidding jams.

In Hand No. 80, Walter's takeout double of one diamond landed him in trouble when North redoubled and East and South passed. Walter started his escape by bidding one heart and when North went to one spade instead of doubling, Walter had escaped again.

Although it is doubtful that this particular North-South

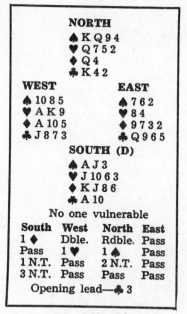

NORTH
♠ K Q 9 4
♥ Q 7 5 2
♦ Q 4
♣ K 4 2

WEST
♠ 10 8 5
♥ A K 9
♦ A 10 5
♣ J 8 7 3

EAST
♠ 7 6 2
♥ 8 4
♦ 9 7 3 2
♣ Q 9 6 5

SOUTH (D)
♠ A J 3
♥ J 10 6 3
♦ K J 8 6
♣ A 10

No one vulnerable

South	West	North	East
1 ♦	Dble.	Rdble.	Pass
Pass	1 ♥	1 ♠	Pass
1 N.T.	Pass	2 N.T.	Pass
3 N.T.	Pass	Pass	Pass

Opening lead—♣ 3

Hand No. 80

would have worked their way to four hearts if left alone, Walter had stopped them from getting to that sure-thing contract and instead had jockeyed them into three no-trump.

Walter's opening lead was the three of clubs. He is old-fashioned and believes in attacking no-trump with his longest suit. East's queen forced South's ace.

South led a heart toward dummy's queen. Walter rose with the king. He pulled in the trick and looked around for a damaging play. He did not expect East to show up with any additional face cards, in view of South's opening bid and the 12 high-card points in dummy. Walter had to do it alone if he wanted to set South. He might set up two club tricks if East held the ten. But there was a better chance. South might hold the ten and East three small clubs.

Out came the jack of clubs, bumping South's ten, and South had to go down.

11

The Slick and the Dead

THERE are a large number of special plays in bridge, and you must use a bag of tricks if you want to be a winner.

The most common of these is the safety play, a move to insure the making of a contract, usually at the expense of an overtrick. The maneuver is a primary tool in rubber bridge, but in match-point contests a player comes up with them when he thinks he is in a good contract, or has received a favorable lead.

South's three no-trump contract in Hand. No. 81 is a bit irregular, as many bids are in duplicate.

After capturing the opening lead of the jack of hearts with his king, South saw that if he could run off his six clubs he would make eleven or possibly twelve tricks. But if he had to lose a club, which was likely, he would score only nine. And if clubs broke 4-0, he might not even make his contract if he played the wrong top club on his first lead.

A perfect safety play was at South's disposal. His problem was whether other players in this match-point game would beat his score if he sacrificed a trick unnecessarily.

He reviewed the bidding and finally decided that his irregular no-trump had shut his opponents out of the bidding. Other Wests might have led a spade, which would be disastrous for no-trump bidders.

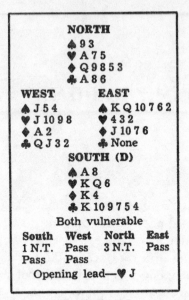

NORTH
♠ 9 3
♥ A 7 5
♦ Q 9 8 5 3
♣ A 8 6

WEST
♠ J 5 4
♥ J 10 9 8
♦ A 2
♣ Q J 3 2

EAST
♠ K Q 10 7 6 2
♥ 4 3 2
♦ J 10 7 6
♣ None

SOUTH (D)
♠ A 8
♥ K Q 6
♦ K 4
♣ K 10 9 7 5 4

Both vulnerable

South	West	North	East
1 N.T.	Pass	3 N.T.	Pass
Pass	Pass		

Opening lead—♥ J

Hand No. 81

South led his four of clubs, West dropped the deuce and South played the six, which took the trick. He knew about the 4-0 break now and still had to lose a club trick, but his contract was safe.

The safety play is not often used in tournament, or duplicate, play. There are finespun differences in the techniques of both types of contract bridge. In rubber bridge you do not gamble with your contract when there is no reason to do so, the small bonus of points for extra tricks is not worth it. But in duplicate a few points may mean a top board and it is occasionally good tactics to gamble sensibly.

The safety play described in the previous hand has a cousin known as the avoidance play, which is something for your kit in both duplicate and rubber bridge. This play, which usually occurs in combination with the loser-on-loser tactic, simply means that you direct things so that the wrong opponent will not get into the lead.

In Hand No. 82, South has been doubled at five hearts and

West has opened the six of spades, which is immediately spotted as a singleton by South.

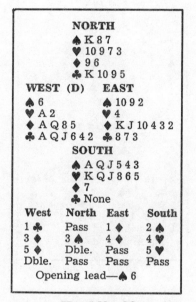

NORTH
♠ K 8 7
♥ 10 9 7 3
♦ 9 6
♣ K 10 9 5

WEST (D)
♠ 6
♥ A 2
♦ A Q 8 5
♣ A Q J 6 4 2

EAST
♠ 10 9 2
♥ 4
♦ K J 10 4 3 2
♣ 8 7 3

SOUTH
♠ A Q J 5 4 3
♥ K Q J 8 6 5
♦ 7
♣ None

West	North	East	South
1 ♣	Pass	1 ♦	2 ♠
3 ♦	3 ♠	4 ♦	4 ♥
5 ♦	Dble.	Pass	5 ♥
Dble.	Pass	Pass	Pass

Opening lead—♠ 6

Hand No. 82

South also surmised that West had the ace and at least one small trump; otherwise the lead of the singleton would have been pointless.

The avoidance play takes place when South wins the trick in dummy and leads his king of clubs. If East produces the ace of clubs, South ruffs and leads a low trump. But East plays small and South discards his losing diamond. (A loser-on-loser.)

West is back in the lead and has no way to put East in.

Hand No. 83 shows another application of the avoidance play, although South failed to use it.

South had two ways to keep out of trouble, and he missed both of them. The first would have been to pass three no-trump. His partner would have made the contract without any trouble

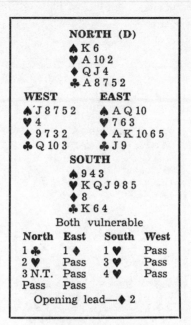

NORTH (D)
♠ K 6
♥ A 10 2
♦ Q J 4
♣ A 8 7 5 2

WEST
♠ J 8 7 5 2
♥ 4
♦ 9 7 3 2
♣ Q 10 3

EAST
♠ A Q 10
♥ 7 6 3
♦ A K 10 6 5
♣ J 9

SOUTH
♠ 9 4 3
♥ K Q J 9 8 5
♦ 8
♣ K 6 4

Both vulnerable

North	East	South	West
1 ♣	1 ♦	1 ♥	Pass
2 ♥	Pass	3 ♥	Pass
3 N.T.	Pass	4 ♥	Pass
Pass	Pass		

Opening lead—♦ 2

Hand No. 83

against a spade or diamond lead, and if play were perfect he could bring home the game against a club or heart lead. The second solution would have been to use the avoidance play.

East won West's opening diamond lead, taking dummy's jack, and shifted to a low trump. South drew trumps and cashed the king of clubs. At this point East made the brilliant play of dropping his jack. The idea was to keep out of the lead. Now West would get into the lead with a club and a spade lead would set the contract.

South could have made an avoidance play by taking the first heart lead in dummy with the ten. Then he could lead his queen of diamonds and discard the club loser from his hand. East would be in with the ace of diamonds and could do anything he wished except set the contract. South would have ruffed out the queen of clubs, drawn trumps, entering dummy with the third trump, and discarded two spades on the long clubs.

Of course a spade opening would have beaten the contract, but West had led to his partner's bid.

In Chapter 9 we discussed various types of finesses, but there is another one, called the obligatory finesse, that is mentioned frequently by bridge players. All technicians have their special languages, and bridge theorists are technicians of a sort. The term "obligatory finesse" sounds like double-talk, but it can be explained by showing it at work in Hand No. 84.

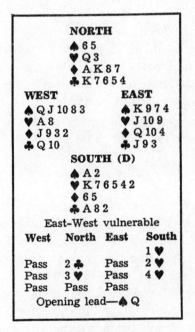

Hand No. 84

South has reached a shaky four-heart contract; when he looks at dummy, and he wishes he had stopped at three. If he is the type who never does anything wrong, he wonders where North dug up the three-heart bid. But at this point the questions are purely academic. He must try to make four hearts.

He must lose a trick in spades and one in clubs, and therefore cannot afford to lose more than one trump.

He plays his ace of spades on West's queen and leads a trump to dummy's queen. It holds after West plays low. Then he leads the three of hearts back toward his hand. East puts on the ten and now comes the obligatory finesse. Obviously East does not hold the ace of trumps because he would have used it to take the first trick. Therefore the ace must be in the West hand. If South plays his king, East will take a second trump trick with his jack. If the jack is in the West hand, South is down anyway, but if the ace is alone, West must play the card.

South plays low. West plays his ace and now South has only to drop East's jack with the king and the contract is home.

We mentioned "loser-on-loser" in connection with the avoidance play. In essence it means that when you have two tricks to lose, try to lose them both at once.

In Hand No. 85, North has a sound raise to two hearts and South has enough power to jump to game, but the cards lie wrong for the declarer; if West opens the jack of spades South will have no play for his contract.

But West opens the top of his diamond sequence instead of playing spades and South covers with dummy's queen. Did West lead from a king-jack-ten combination? East produces the king to answer that question and South now must proceed cautiously if he wants to make his contract.

South lets the king of diamonds hold, but East leads diamonds back and South plays his ace. After drawing trumps, South plays clubs, hoping they will break, but they do not.

South must use loser-on-loser to make his contract. He leads dummy's last club, East plays his jack and South discards a spade from his own hand.

East is in the lead with the second defensive trick and he must lead either a spade or a diamond. A spade makes dummy's king good and a diamond allows South to discard one of the two remaining spades from his hand and ruff in dummy.

All of the trick-stretching gimmicks in bridge are not the

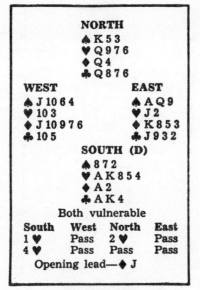

NORTH
♠ K 5 3
♥ Q 9 7 6
♦ Q 4
♣ Q 8 7 6

WEST
♠ J 10 6 4
♥ 10 3
♦ J 10 9 7 6
♣ 10 5

EAST
♠ A Q 9
♥ J 2
♦ K 8 5 3
♣ J 9 3 2

SOUTH (D)
♠ 8 7 2
♥ A K 8 5 4
♦ A 2
♣ A K 4

Both vulnerable

South	West	North	East
1 ♥	Pass	2 ♥	Pass
4 ♥	Pass	Pass	Pass

Opening lead—♦ J

Hand No. 85

exclusive property of the declarer. There are weapons that may also be used by the defense.

The uppercut is a defensive weapon in contract bridge. Its use is described in Hand No. 86, which came to us from the monthly bulletin of the Johannesburg Bridge Club, contributed by Ben Cohen of Hove, South Africa.

Mr. Cohen points out that one of the rules of defense is never to give declarer a ruff and a discard, such as was pointed out in Hand No. 85, but that there are exceptions to all rules.

In this hand South's preemptive jump to four spades shut West out of the bidding. West has no problem in pulling in three club tricks. His next idea is to find another trick that will set South.

The declarer bid four spades all by himself and must have at least six. Since South has played three clubs, he cannot have more than four red cards in his hand. Dummy has the top cards in the red suits.

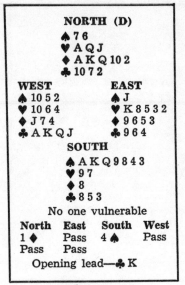

NORTH (D)
♠ 7 6
♥ A Q J
♦ A K Q 10 2
♣ 10 7 2

WEST
♠ 10 5 2
♥ 10 6 4
♦ J 7 4
♣ A K Q J

EAST
♠ J
♥ K 8 5 3 2
♦ 9 6 5 3
♣ 9 6 4

SOUTH
♠ A K Q 9 8 4 3
♥ 9 7
♦ 8
♣ 8 5 3

No one vulnerable

North	East	South	West
1 ♦	Pass	4 ♠	Pass
Pass	Pass		

Opening lead—♣ K

Hand No. 86

The only possible trick is in trumps — if West can make his ten good by driving out a high honor with an uppercut — assuming that South's spades are not so strong as to have all four honors.

He hopes to get his partner to ruff the lead of a fourth club with a face-card. He doesn't know if East has one, but it is the only chance to set the hand.

West leads his last club and if East is smart he will use his jack, uppercutting South and forcing him to use a high honor. West's ten will take the setting trick.

Some bridge devices resemble maneuvers of chess in that they set up a threat to one line of action and force the opponent to do something else, often less damaging. One of these tactics is the Bath coup.

The Bath coup dates back to the days of whist. Some writers say it was named for the Earl of Bath, who they presume named the play. Actually the term is derived from the town of Bath, a seaside resort in England where the play was first made in the last century before contract, or even auction, bridge was invented.

Unlike other coups, which can take varied forms, the Bath coup is a specific play. Hand No. 87, played by Andy Gabrilovich of Washington, illustrates the play beautifully.

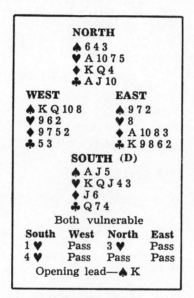

NORTH
♠ 6 4 3
♥ A 10 7 5
♦ K Q 4
♣ A J 10

WEST
♠ K Q 10 8
♥ 9 6 2
♦ 9 7 5 2
♣ 5 3

EAST
♠ 9 7 2
♥ 8
♦ A 10 8 3
♣ K 9 8 6 2

SOUTH (D)
♠ A J 5
♥ K Q J 4 3
♦ J 6
♣ Q 7 4

Both vulnerable

South	West	North	East
1 ♥	Pass	3 ♥	Pass
4 ♥	Pass	Pass	Pass

Opening lead—♠ K

Hand No. 87

West opened the king of spades against a four-heart contract. Andy, sitting South, let it hold.

That, specifically, is the Bath coup: Hold off a king lead with ace-jack and one or more small cards. If the suit is continued, you make either your ace or your jack. Therefore the opponent must shift, which gives declarer time to develop some other suit.

West shifted to the five of clubs, after noting that his partner played the deuce of spades — a signal discouraging the suit.

Andy refused the club finesse because he had more important things to do. He pulled trumps and knocked out the ace of diamonds. East made a spade return after taking the ace, and Andy played his ace of spades. Later he discarded his jack of spades on one of dummy's high diamonds.

Andy had to lose a trick to the king of clubs, but the defense got only one diamond, one spade and one club, not enough to set the contract.

We will discuss squeeze plays later on, but there is a particular form of squeeze known as the Vienna coup, which deserves a place in this chapter on specialized play.

Hand No. 88 shows this coup, in which the declarer begins by setting up a trick in an opponent's hand and then squeezes him.

The original Vienna coup was given as a double dummy problem and it took a little time before anyone was able to solve it. Today, every good player keeps this coup in his handy kit.

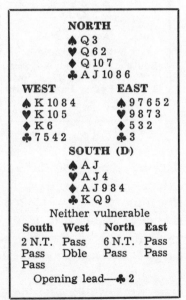

NORTH
♠ Q 3
♥ Q 6 2
♦ Q 10 7
♣ A J 10 8 6

WEST
♠ K 10 8 4
♥ K 10 5
♦ K 6
♣ 7 5 4 2

EAST
♠ 9 7 6 5 2
♥ 9 8 7 3
♦ 5 3 2
♣ 3

SOUTH (D)
♠ A J
♥ A J 4
♦ A J 9 8 4
♣ K Q 9

Neither vulnerable

South	West	North	East
2 N.T.	Pass	6 N.T.	Pass
Pass	Dble	Pass	Pass
Pass			

Opening lead—♣ 2

Hand No. 88

South actually did not have quite enough strength for a two no-trump opening and North's jump to six represented all his values and possibly a trifle more. But the hands fit and the six no-trump is a very good contract.

If the diamond finesse worked, South would have his slam. Even if it did not work, South had only to find one other king in the East hand to make six. He didn't like the idea of guessing, and, as you see, all the kings were wrong. South would have gone down if West had not come through with a very bad double.

The double strongly indicated that West held all three kings and the Vienna coup seemed to be the best and easiest way to meet the threat.

South won the first club with dummy's ten of clubs and lost the diamond finesse. West led another club, which South won in his own hand. Then he ran off the rest of the diamond suit, discarding a small heart and the queen of hearts from dummy.

Next South cashed has ace of spades, setting up the king in West's hand, and ran the rest of the club suit.

The last club lead forced West to unguard his king of hearts in order to hang on to his king of spades. South made the last two tricks with the ace and jack of hearts.

Unblocking is a tactic most players use as a matter of course. Hand No. 89 is a sensational example of its use.

The unblock was used as a defensive measure, which makes it even more unusual because it is something that is usually overlooked. The hand was played by the late Harry Harkavy, sitting West, and Cliff Russell of Miami Beach, in the East spot. As a team both players were very successful in tournament play all over the country, and a large part of their success was the result of complete partnership confidence.

Defending against a part-score contract of two spades, Harry opened the king of hearts and continued with the ace, in spite of Cliff's signal to stop by dropping the four.

Declarer ruffed and led a club, which Harry won with his ace. A third heart was won in dummy and the ace of spades was played.

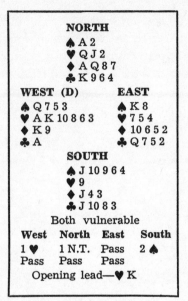

NORTH
♠ A 2
♥ Q J 2
♦ A Q 8 7
♣ K 9 6 4

WEST (D)
♠ Q 7 5 3
♥ A K 10 8 6 3
♦ K 9
♣ A

EAST
♠ K 8
♥ 7 5 4
♦ 10 6 5 2
♣ Q 7 5 2

SOUTH
♠ J 10 9 6 4
♥ 9
♦ J 4 3
♣ J 10 8 3

Both vulnerable

West	North	East	South
1 ♥	1 N.T.	Pass	2 ♠
Pass	Pass	Pass	

Opening lead—♥ K

Hand No. 89

At this point Cliff came up with a tremendous defensive play. He dropped his king of spades on the ace.

Occasions occur when a player should unblock with a king, but when the card is the king of trumps these times are infrequent — which, to put it mildly, is an understatement. This, however, was one of these occasions. Had Cliff clung to his king he would have been thrown into the lead. He could only have led a diamond or club to dummy. Of course, a combination of a diamond lead and the play of the nine by West would have beaten the hand, but the unblock was certain.

Declarer led a second trump, which Harry won with his queen. Now Harry led hearts at every opportunity and South could bring home only two diamonds and his last two trumps. Added to the three tricks he had already pulled in, he was one trick short.

When the contract is in no-trump, the strategy often differs from that of a suit contract.

Most no-trump contracts make or go down after a race between declarer and the defenders to establish low cards in long suits.

In Hand No. 90, West's queen of spades opening is in full accord with this principle. He has a suit he hopes to establish in two leads and he has the ace of hearts as an entry.

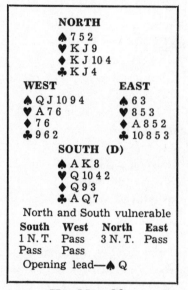

```
            NORTH
          ♠ 7 5 2
          ♥ K J 9
          ♦ K J 10 4
          ♣ K J 4
 WEST                   EAST
♠ Q J 10 9 4          ♠ 6 3
♥ A 7 6              ♥ 8 5 3
♦ 7 6               ♦ A 8 5 2
♣ 9 6 2             ♣ 10 8 5 3
            SOUTH (D)
          ♠ A K 8
          ♥ Q 10 4 2
          ♦ Q 9 3
          ♣ A Q 7
```

North and South vulnerable

South	West	North	East
1 N. T.	Pass	3 N. T.	Pass
Pass	Pass		

Opening lead—♠ Q

Hand No. 90

South does not know where the red aces are, but he needs tricks in both red suits if he is to make his contract. He also knows that if West holds five spades and both red aces, the contract is doomed. However, if spades break 4-3, West will get only two spade tricks and his two aces and South will win the race.

Next South considers a 5-2 spade break, which is actually the holding. If aces are split he must knock out the right ace first, or he will be down.

If South were clairvoyant, he would lead hearts, knock out the ace and make five no-trump. But South might just as easily lead diamonds after taking the first trick. East would be in the lead, back would come a spade and South's defense against West's long suit would be destroyed with the heart ace outstanding.

South should resort to ducking. He would not take the first spade trick, but the second. Then no matter which opponent got in after he led a red suit, South would be safe. If South knocked out the ace of hearts first, everything would be fine. If he knocked out the ace of diamonds first or last, East would have no more spades to lead. South would make only four, but he would be certain of his contract.

In no-trump or suit contracts you hope for an advantageous lead when your opponent captures a trick. Sometimes you have an opportunity to insure this type of lead by eliminating the other suits so that your bridge foe will be forced to lead what you want.

In an elimination play declarer exhausts an opponent's off suits so that he will have to make a favorable lead for declarer. Hand No. 91 was played in a York, Pennsylvania, regional tournament a few years ago.

Most South players reached six spades on this hand, and almost all of them took the club finesse and went down. But Col. Bill Christian of Staten Island made the slam by using an elimination play. Of course the play might not have worked, but Bill still had the finesse to fall back on.

He started by winning the diamond opening and ruffing a diamond. Then he cashed his ace of hearts, noting that West dropped the ten. Two leads pulled trumps and left Bill in dummy.

He discarded a club on dummy's last high diamond, led a heart and played the eight from his hand. West had to win with the queen and Bill's eliminator had done its job.

West had no hearts or trumps and had to play clubs or diamonds. If he led a club, Bill had a free finesse through the East hand. If West led a diamond, Bill would ruff in dummy and

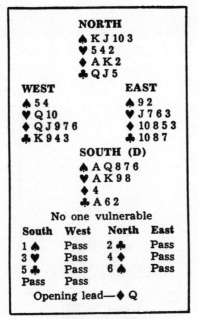

NORTH
♠ K J 10 3
♥ 5 4 2
♦ A K 2
♣ Q J 5

WEST
♠ 5 4
♥ Q 10
♦ Q J 9 7 6
♣ K 9 4 3

EAST
♠ 9 2
♥ J 7 6 3
♦ 10 8 5 3
♣ 10 8 7

SOUTH (D)
♠ A Q 8 7 6
♥ A K 9 8
♦ 4
♣ A 6 2

No one vulnerable

South	West	North	East
1 ♠	Pass	2 ♣	Pass
3 ♥	Pass	4 ♦	Pass
5 ♣	Pass	6 ♠	Pass
Pass	Pass		

Opening lead—♦ Q

Hand No. 91

toss his losing club on the trick as a discard from his hand.

These same principles are also used in an end play. You whittle the enemy down to his last cards, then throw him in so that he will have to make a lead that is advantageous to you.

Hand No. 92 was sent to us by Dr. Nathan Divinsky of the University of British Columbia. The fact that the contract was a prosaic two hearts does not detract from this hand's interest because it was a duplicate game and Dr. Divinsky made an overtrick, which meant a lot in the game.

West opened the king of spades, followed with the ace and a third spade, which was taken by dummy's queen. Then Dr. Divinsky cashed the king of hearts and entered his own hand with the ace. He led a club, which was won by dummy's king, and East was thrown into the lead with a heart.

East made the best play, a diamond lead. South's jack forced

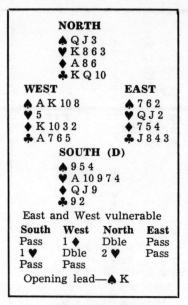

NORTH
♠ Q J 3
♥ K 8 6 3
♦ A 8 6
♣ K Q 10

WEST
♠ A K 10 8
♥ 5
♦ K 10 3 2
♣ A 7 6 5

EAST
♠ 7 6 2
♥ Q J 2
♦ 7 5 4
♣ J 8 4 3

SOUTH (D)
♠ 9 5 4
♥ A 10 9 7 4
♦ Q J 9
♣ 9 2

East and West vulnerable

South	West	North	East
Pass	1 ♦	Dble	Pass
1 ♥	Dble	2 ♥	Pass
Pass	Pass		

Opening lead—♠ K

Hand No. 92

West's king, which was taken by dummy's ace. Now Dr. Divinsky led a trump, which forced West to make his third discard. He had already jettisoned a club and a diamond on the second and third trump leads and now he dropped his last low club. He still held the thirteenth spade as an exit card, but Dr. D. took care of that by playing his own last trump. West could not afford to unguard the ten of diamonds or throw the ace of clubs, and the spade had to go.

Now the time had come for the end play. A club put West in the lead and he had to lead away from his ten of diamonds.

Once in a while, the cards will win for you without any fancy tactics, if you give them a chance. On other occasions, letting the cards play for the breaks is a necessity, as in Hand No. 93.

North's jump to three no-trump was correct, even though he has only 8 high-card points. He expected his seven-card diamond suit to be of great help to his partner. Expert South had opened an irregular no-trump with a worthless doubleton. (Every expert does this, but they are not supposed to.)

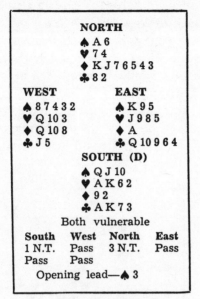

NORTH
♠ A 6
♥ 7 4
♦ K J 7 6 5 4 3
♣ 8 2

WEST
♠ 8 7 4 3 2
♥ Q 10 3
♦ Q 10 8
♣ J 5

EAST
♠ K 9 5
♥ J 9 8 5
♦ A
♣ Q 10 9 6 4

SOUTH (D)
♠ Q J 10
♥ A K 6 2
♦ 9 2
♣ A K 7 3

Both vulnerable

South	West	North	East
1 N.T.	Pass	3 N.T.	Pass
Pass	Pass		

Opening lead—♠ 3

Hand No. 93

East won the first spade with the king and a spade return killed off the entry to the diamond suit.

At this point, South reminded himself never again to open worthless doubleton no-trumps, but it was too late to do anything about this one. But just as he was feeling repentant, he suddenly experienced a faint glow of hope. Not much of a chance, to be sure, but beggars can't choose, and South was begging.

He crossed to his hand with a heart and led the nine of diamonds. West covered with the ten and South ducked in dummy. East had to play his singleton ace.

South won the spade return, led his deuce of diamonds and finessed successfully against West's queen — as who wouldn't — and made five-odd. He also canceled the reminder not to bid no-trump again with a worthless doubleton.

The point is that the only chance South had to win was to find a singleton ace in the East hand. He gave the cards a chance and the chance was indeed his best play.

Almost a corollary of "give the cards a chance" is "give the other side a chance to go wrong." A few years ago, Oswald Jacoby ran a bidding contest; first prize was a trip to the Hawaiian regionals where the winner played as Ozzie's partner in every event for which they would be eligible. The winner was Bob Marks of Vista, California.

The most difficult part of bridge is defense, due partly to the fact that the declarer has most of the advantages. Hand No. 94 was one of the first hands Ozzie and Bob played, and Bob came up with a beautiful play.

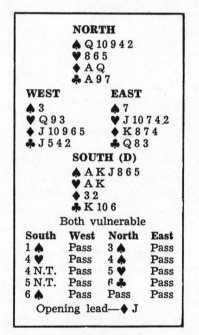

	NORTH		
	♠ Q 10 9 4 2		
	♥ 8 6 5		
	♦ A Q		
	♣ A 9 7		
WEST		**EAST**	
♠ 3		♠ 7	
♥ Q 9 3		♥ J 10 7 4 2	
♦ J 10 9 6 5		♦ K 8 7 4	
♣ J 5 4 2		♣ Q 8 3	
	SOUTH (D)		
	♠ A K J 8 6 5		
	♥ A K		
	♦ 3 2		
	♣ K 10 6		

Both vulnerable

South	West	North	East
1 ♠	Pass	3 ♠	Pass
4 ♥	Pass	4 ♠	Pass
4 N.T.	Pass	5 ♥	Pass
5 N.T.	Pass	6 ♣	Pass
6 ♠	Pass	Pass	Pass

Opening lead—♦ J

Hand No. 94

Ozzie, sitting West, opened the jack of diamonds against South's six-spade contract. South went up with dummy's ace after a little thought. He drew trumps, cashed his ace and king of hearts, ruffed a heart, and entered dummy with a second trump. Then he threw Bob into the lead with the king of diamonds.

This was a standard elimination play, which we discussed in Hand No. 91. Bob could lead a heart and give South a ruff and a discard, or he could lead a club. Most players would avoid the heart trap and lead a low club, whereupon Ozzie's jack would fall under dummy's ace and declarer would finesse successfully against Bob's queen.

But Bob had already foreseen the situation and he came up with the play that would give the declarer a chance to go wrong. He led the queen of clubs.

South took a couple of seconds to get his balance and then he began to think, which is sometimes bad. Had Bob led the queen from a queen-jack holding? If that were the case, South had to win in dummy and finesse against the jack in Bob's hand. But, if Bob had led the queen from nothing, as was the case, declarer should win in his own hand and finesse for the jack in Ozzie's hand.

Declarer had a fifty-fifty chance to guess wrong because he could not see all the cards. He overlooked the reason for Bob's lead — to give South a chance to make a mistake. He decided Bob had led from queen-jack and took the queen with dummy's ace. With Ozzie's jack behind the king-ten, the slam was set.

12

The Card Squeezer

ANY child who plays the simplest of games knows that the ace will take a king. And with that as a basic fact, it follows that in order to make a king safe from an ace the king must have a small card to protect it when the ace is played.

This is the factor in the squeeze. Also very important is the ability to count cards. Before we illustrate types of squeeze plays, we will show a few examples of card-counting.

The late P. Hal Sims stood three inches over six feet and weighed 350 pounds, but he stood even taller and weighed more among bridge players in the late 'twenties, when he was unquestionably the best auction-bridge player in the world. Card-counting was just as important as in contract bridge, but in those first days of the game he refused to concede that scientific bidding was necessary.

In Hand No. 95, Hal's jump to seven no-trump was typical of his slam bidding, but the contract was a good one. He could count twelve top tricks and could make the thirteenth if spades broke 3-3. Failing that, he could still fall back on a finesse for the king of hearts.

Look at the cards and note that West held the singleton king of hearts and that spades do not break. It looks as if one peek would have been worth more than two finesses, but Hal plucked that king just as easily as if he had looked into his opponent's hand.

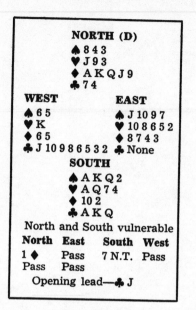

NORTH (D)
♠ 8 4 3
♥ J 9 3
♦ A K Q J 9
♣ 7 4

WEST
♠ 6 5
♥ K
♦ 6 5
♣ J 10 9 8 6 5 3 2

EAST
♠ J 10 9 7
♥ 10 8 6 5 2
♦ 8 7 4 3
♣ None

SOUTH
♠ A K Q 2
♥ A Q 7 4
♦ 10 2
♣ A K Q

North and South vulnerable

North	East	South	West
1 ♦	Pass	7 N.T.	Pass
Pass	Pass		

Opening lead—♣ J

Hand No. 95

It was all a matter of counting the cards. After he took the jack of clubs, he tried the spades and noted that West held only two. Then he played diamonds and, when West showed out on the third lead, Hal had counted twelve of his cards. (East had shown out on the first lead of clubs.) He knew that the other card in West's hand had to be a heart.

On the last diamond lead, East had discarded down to one heart in order to hang on to the jack of spades. Hal discarded his deuce of spades and made the last two tricks with the ace and queen of hearts. It did not matter whether East or West held the king.

Hand No. 96 shows another no-trump grand slam manufactured out of a count of cards.

South looked over dummy carefully and counted twelve top tricks at no-trump with a two-way finesse for the queen of hearts. He had to take the finesse, but the correct technique was to ac-

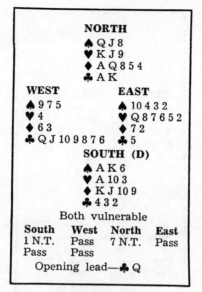

NORTH
♠ Q J 8
♥ K J 9
♦ A Q 8 5 4
♣ A K

WEST
♠ 9 7 5
♥ 4
♦ 6 3
♣ Q J 10 9 8 7 6

EAST
♠ 10 4 3 2
♥ Q 8 7 6 5 2
♦ 7 2
♣ 5

SOUTH (D)
♠ A K 6
♥ A 10 3
♦ K J 10 9
♣ 4 3 2

Both vulnerable

South	West	North	East
1 N.T.	Pass	7 N.T.	Pass
Pass	Pass		

Opening lead—♣ Q

Hand No. 96

quire as much information as possible before he attempted it.

He won the opening club lead, and cashed the next nine tricks in spades, diamonds and clubs.

East discarded on the second club, showing a singleton. Therefore West had started with seven in this suit. West followed to three spades and two diamonds, showing he had at most a singleton heart. Therefore, South led a heart from his hand. West played the four, and South knew where the queen was hiding. He took the trick with the king in dummy, led to his ace and finessed for the queen with complete safety.

The plays in the above hands were not real squeezes. The squeeze is a simple play, not merely a tool of the expert, and the basic requirement is to be able to recognize a squeeze situation. No doubt many people who are mystified by this play have worked it without realizing they have done so.

Hand No. 97 looks like bad news for South after two leads of hearts from West and a ruff of a third heart by East. South still has a club to lose.

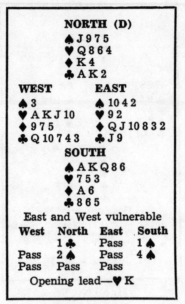

NORTH (D)
♠ J 9 7 5
♥ Q 8 6 4
♦ K 4
♣ A K 2

WEST
♠ 3
♥ A K J 10
♦ 9 7 5
♣ Q 10 7 4 3

EAST
♠ 10 4 2
♥ 9 2
♦ Q J 10 8 3 2
♣ J 9

SOUTH
♠ A K Q 8 6
♥ 7 5 3
♦ A 6
♣ 8 6 5

East and West vulnerable

West	North	East	South
	1 ♣	Pass	1 ♠
Pass	2 ♠	Pass	4 ♠
Pass	Pass	Pass	

Opening lead—♥ K

Hand No. 97

At this point, while East was leading a diamond, South recognizes a squeeze situation. Dummy's fourth heart is a threat against West, who holds the ten, and dummy's third club will also be a threat, if West holds five or more clubs.

South won the diamond in dummy and pulled trump with three leads. When West discarded two clubs, South began to have hope.

Next South played the ace of diamonds, then led a fourth trump. West discarded a low diamond. South led his last trump and West had run out of discards. If West plays the ten of hearts, dummy's eight will take the last trick. If West plays the ten of clubs, dummy's deuce of clubs will be a winner.

There was nothing West could do about it.

A classic squeeze situation is illustrated in Hand No. 98.

South has twelve top tricks and there is a potential thirteenth in clubs or diamonds. If either suit breaks 3-3, a squeeze is not

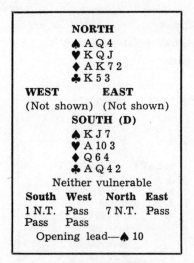

```
                NORTH
              ♠ A Q 4
              ♥ K Q J
              ♦ A K 7 2
              ♣ K 5 3
WEST              EAST
(Not shown)  (Not shown)
              SOUTH (D)
              ♠ K J 7
              ♥ A 10 3
              ♦ Q 6 4
              ♣ A Q 4 2
         Neither vulnerable
South   West   North   East
1 N.T.  Pass   7 N.T.  Pass
Pass    Pass
      Opening lead—♠ 10
```

Hand No. 98

necessary. If one opponent is long in both suits, he can be squeezed out of one stopper or the other.

A simple line of play is to cash all the spades and hearts in the hands immediately. Then everyone will have seven cards, but it takes eight cards for one man to stop both minor suits and the squeeze has operated — provided one man started with long clubs *and* long diamonds. You will lose if each is long in one of the minor suits.

But the expert may increase his chances by giving his opponents an opportunity to go wrong. Neither of the opponents can see the fourth club in the South hand. Both see the fourth diamond.

There is no hope for deception in diamonds, but expert South starts proceedings by winning the spade with dummy's queen and dropping his seven. Then he runs off three diamonds and three hearts. If one opponent had started with four clubs and four spades, he would have to discard one black card.

He probably would not throw a club, but he might do so.

That type of deception constitutes what is known as a pseudo-squeeze. There was no real squeeze, but a defender let himself be squeezed anyway.

Hand No. 99 shows what Walter Wyman of Boston named the submarine squeeze.

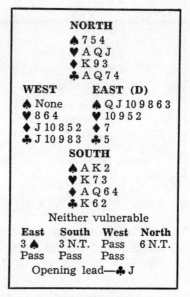

NORTH
♠ 7 5 4
♥ A Q J
♦ K 9 3
♣ A Q 7 4

WEST
♠ None
♥ 8 6 4
♦ J 10 8 5 2
♣ J 10 9 8 3

EAST (D)
♠ Q J 10 9 8 6 3
♥ 10 9 5 2
♦ 7
♣ 5

SOUTH
♠ A K 2
♥ K 7 3
♦ A Q 6 4
♣ K 6 2

Neither vulnerable

East	South	West	North
3 ♠	3 N.T.	Pass	6 N.T.
Pass	Pass	Pass	

Opening lead—♣ J

Hand No. 99

East's opening three-spade bid helped North and South get to six no-trump. After West's lead of the jack of clubs, it seemed that only eleven tricks were available. But South hoped to find one in spades, clubs or diamonds.

In order to develop the squeeze, South must give away a trick so that all but one of his cards will be winners. This is known as "rectifying the count." But he does not do this immediately. It won't hurt to see if either minor suit will break first.

South plays two clubs. East shows out on the second round. South plays two diamonds and East again shows that he held a singleton in this suit. South knows he must try to squeeze West, who started with five cards in each minor suit.

If South plays his top hearts and spades at this point no

squeeze will develop because West has two extra cards to discard — one club and one diamond — and he can still take two
tricks.

Hence the submarine play: South leads his deuce of spades.
East is in the lead and must return either a heart or a spade.
West has to discard a heart on the spade lead. No matter what
East returns now, West will have to throw away a card in one
long suit after South plays his three top hearts. North's fourth
club or South's fourth diamond will take the final trick, depending on West's discard after the hearts and spades are all played.

Albert (Dingy) Weiss played one of the best hands in the 1965
trials when he made a slightly unsound four-spade contract. He
sat South in Hand No. 100.

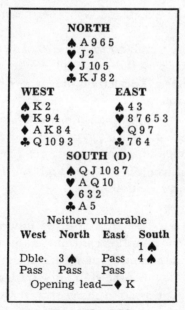

NORTH
♠ A 9 6 5
♥ J 2
♦ J 10 5
♣ K J 8 2

WEST
♠ K 2
♥ K 9 4
♦ A K 8 4
♣ Q 10 9 3

EAST
♠ 4 3
♥ 8 7 6 5 3
♦ Q 9 7
♣ 7 6 4

SOUTH (D)
♠ Q J 10 8 7
♥ A Q 10
♦ 6 3 2
♣ A 5

Neither vulnerable

West	North	East	South
			1 ♠
Dble.	3 ♠	Pass	4 ♠
Pass	Pass	Pass	

Opening lead—♦ K

Hand No. 100

Everyone else stopped at three spades and made it exactly,
while Weiss made four. "No trouble," Dingy said; "they took
the first three tricks and I took the next ten."

Those ten tricks represented some nice card-counting and a squeeze.

Weiss knew his four-spade bid was a decided push. North's jump to three spades over West's takeout double was not forcing, but Weiss hoped his partner would not hold three small diamonds, which North did.

West opened the king of diamonds, continued with the ace, and then played the eight. After East took the third trick with his queen of diamonds, he returned a heart.

It seemed certain that the king of hearts would be in the West hand, since West would need it for his double, and Weiss went up with his ace. His next step was to finesse successfully against the king of spades. Then he ran off the rest of his trumps and discarded everything but four clubs in dummy. In his hand, Weiss retained the queen and one other heart and the ace and one other club.

West had to let a club go in order to hang on to his king of hearts. Now Weiss played the ace and another club and finessed against West's queen. This left dummy with two good clubs and Weiss with his game.

Most squeezes aren't game-or-set matters. Sometimes a squeeze simply produces an overtrick for an easy contract. Many times a squeeze will develop at a mere part score. The first thing to remember about squeezes is that *any time you have all the tricks but one, there is a potential squeeze.*

The next step is to cash all your sure winners in other suits in order to squeeze the guarding cards into a discard. In Hand No. 101, South ruffs the second diamond and then runs a few rounds of trumps. Then he takes the club finesse, which loses, and East returns a heart. At this point many players would try to break the clubs and settle for four-odd when they failed to break. A try for a squeeze risks nothing and produces the overtrick.

South leads a second club to dummy and ruffs a third diamond. This move is essential because South does not want East to spoil the little plan by hanging on to a high diamond.

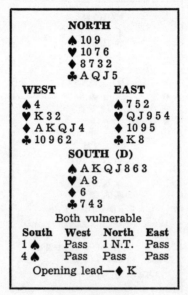

NORTH
♠ 10 9
♥ 10 7 6
♦ 8 7 3 2
♣ A Q J 5

WEST
♠ 4
♥ K 3 2
♦ A K Q J 4
♣ 10 9 6 2

EAST
♠ 7 5 2
♥ Q J 9 5 4
♦ 10 9 5
♣ K 8

SOUTH (D)
♠ A K Q J 8 6 3
♥ A 8
♦ 6
♣ 7 4 3

Both vulnerable

South	West	North	East
1 ♠	Pass	1 N.T.	Pass
4 ♠	Pass	Pass	Pass

Opening lead—♦ K

Hand No. 101

Now South runs off his trumps. He does *not* run off all but one, but *every trump he has* — because West will not be squeezed until the last trump is led.

Then, and not before, West must hold on to a high diamond or sacrifice the one club that will prevent his ten from falling under dummy's jack.

If West discards a diamond, South discards a low club from dummy. If West throws off a club, South tosses his diamond from dummy. In either case, the two cards remaining in dummy are winners.

Many squeeze situations depend on the declarer's ability to count the hands of the opponents. Almost all squeeze end-plays fall into this category.

In Hand No. 102, West opens hearts against a four-spade contract by South and continues until declarer ruffs the third round. South leads a trump to dummy, ruffs out the last heart from that hand and plays a second spade to dummy.

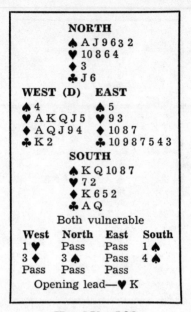

NORTH
♠ A J 9 6 3 2
♥ 10 8 6 4
♦ 3
♣ J 6

WEST (D)
♠ 4
♥ A K Q J 5
♦ A Q J 9 4
♣ K 2

EAST
♠ 5
♥ 9 3
♦ 10 8 7
♣ 10 9 8 7 5 4 3

SOUTH
♠ K Q 10 8 7
♥ 7 2
♦ K 6 5 2
♣ A Q

Both vulnerable

West	North	East	South
1 ♥	Pass	Pass	1 ♠
3 ♦	3 ♠	Pass	4 ♠
Pass	Pass	Pass	

Opening lead—♥ K

Hand No. 102

South suspects that West holds the ace of diamonds and probably the king of clubs, for West made a strong bid on the second round, indicating a powerful hand. East has been silent and probably has a bust hand.

If South throws West into the lead, South might force West eventually to lead from his king of clubs. However, putting West in the lead is difficult. If South leads a diamond from dummy, East is likely to have a card high enough to break things up.

But South can see a squeeze situation. He runs off all dummy's trumps and keeps the singleton king of diamonds and the ace-queen of clubs in his own hand.

While doing this, South watches West's discards carefully. West must discard down to his ace of diamonds if he is to maintain a guard for his king of clubs. Now South leads a diamond and West is in the lead with the ace. He can do nothing but lose his king of clubs, because he must lead a club. If West unguards his king, hoping that South will finesse, South, who has kept track of the cards, simply cashes his ace and queen.

An expert West, however, may keep a guard for his king of clubs and try to discard deceptively in diamonds. He is likely to discard the nine of diamonds, then the deuce of clubs, finally the queen and jack of diamonds, hanging on to the four. South may well be fooled and assume that West has the singleton ace of diamonds and the guarded king of clubs.

13

Grand Larceny

IN the first twelve chapters, we have shown examples of good and bad play, but throughout we have tried to emphasize one thing: to play winning bridge, you must use your wits. We have shown how perverse luck can be, and how determining what cards are in what hand is sometimes a matter of sheer guess.

Thinking will show you when it is necessary to disregard the "book plays." It is dangerous not to play according to established standards, but in bridge you must sometimes take risks. Even the experts often toss away the book and bid unsoundly. When they manage to extricate themselves from some of these undertakings, they talk about it for years.

As in all games, you can sometimes win with a fake play. You can make a psychic bid, false-card, underlead an ace, or do anything permitted by the official rules of contract bridge to deceive an opponent. But you must remember that your partner may also be fooled.

A couple of examples of false-carding have been demonstrated, and now we'll study the procedure. False-carding is as old as card games themselves. One of the prettiest examples we have seen was made by Charley Dunaif in a rubber-bridge game at New York's Whist Club a few years ago, as shown in Hand No. 103.

Charley was playing East against a six-spade contract by

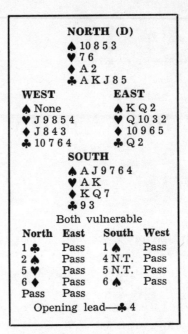

NORTH (D)
♠ 10 8 5 3
♥ 7 6
♦ A 2
♣ A K J 8 5

WEST
♠ None
♥ J 9 8 5 4
♦ J 8 4 3
♣ 10 7 6 4

EAST
♠ K Q 2
♥ Q 10 3 2
♦ 10 9 6 5
♣ Q 2

SOUTH
♠ A J 9 7 6 4
♥ A K
♦ K Q 7
♣ 9 3

Both vulnerable

North	East	South	West
1 ♣	Pass	1 ♠	Pass
2 ♠	Pass	4 N.T.	Pass
5 ♥	Pass	5 N.T.	Pass
6 ♦	Pass	6 ♠	Pass
Pass	Pass		

Opening lead—♣ 4

Hand No. 103

South. At this contract, South has an automatic trump safety play. He would lead low from dummy's trumps. When East followed low, in this case with the deuce, South would play low to guard against the possibility that all three trumps are in the East hand.

This hand opened with West leading the four of clubs. The king was played from dummy.

Charley had listened to the bidding and noted that South had tried to get to a grand slam. Hence South would have no losers, except in the trump suit. South was a good player, and Charley knew that with ten trumps, South should take the safety play. With nine trumps, South would take two finesses.

Charley had to do something about that normal safety play and at this moment he did it. He dropped the queen of clubs under dummy's king. He did not pull the wrong card; dropping the queen was his answer to the problem.

South led the ten of spades from dummy. Charley played the deuce. Now South went into deep thought. Should he or should he not make the safety play? He finally convinced himself he could not afford it. If West held either the king or the queen of trumps, and thus got in the lead, West would lead a club and Charley would trump. South was assuming, of course, that Charley would not have dropped the queen unless it was a singleton club. South went up with the ace of spades and Charley made his two high trumps winners. The contract was down one.

When declarer leads one of equals (king-queen, queen-jack, or some other adjacent combination below the ace), he usually leads the higher; thus the lead of some other card is a form of false-carding.

The late Spottswood Bowers of New York once obtained a very interesting result from this type of play.

On the four-spade contract in Hand No. 104, Spotty took West's opening lead of the queen of diamonds in his hand with the ace.

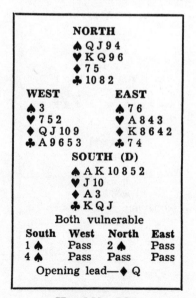

```
               NORTH
               ♠ Q J 9 4
               ♥ K Q 9 6
               ♦ 7 5
               ♣ 10 8 2
   WEST                      EAST
   ♠ 3                       ♠ 7 6
   ♥ 7 5 2                   ♥ A 8 4 3
   ♦ Q J 10 9               ♦ K 8 6 4 2
   ♣ A 9 6 5 3              ♣ 7 4
               SOUTH (D)
               ♠ A K 10 8 5 2
               ♥ J 10
               ♦ A 3
               ♣ K Q J
          Both vulnerable
   South   West    North    East
   1 ♠     Pass    2 ♠      Pass
   4 ♠     Pass    Pass     Pass
       Opening lead—♦ Q
```

Hand No. 104

Then he led a trump to dummy's queen and returned with a low trump to his ace.

His next play was the ten of hearts, which he covered with dummy's queen. This gave East the impression that West held the jack of hearts, and East ducked. Next Spotty led the six of hearts from dummy and again East held back with his ace, while Spotty cashed his jack.

He led a trump back to dummy's nine and played the king of hearts. Now East played his ace, but it was too late. Spotty ruffed, led another low trump to dummy's jack and discarded the three of diamonds on dummy's nine of hearts. He wound up losing only one trick.

The extra tricks didn't mean a lot, because the game was rubber bridge, but it shows how you can take three tricks in a suit to your opponents' none, even though they hold the ace.

Hand No. 105 shows how an expert can come up with a brilliant play, if given the chance to make it.

```
                    NORTH
                    ♠ A
                    ♥ 10 6 2
                    ♦ J 9 8 7 2
                    ♣ A K Q 6
        WEST (D)                EAST
        ♠ 3                     ♠ 10 7 6 4
        ♥ 8 7 5 4 3             ♥ A K J
        ♦ A K                   ♦ Q 10 6 3
        ♣ J 10 9 5 3            ♣ 7 4
                    SOUTH
                    ♠ K Q J 9 8 5 2
                    ♥ Q 9
                    ♦ 5 4
                    ♣ 8 2
        North and South vulnerable
        West    North    East    South
        Pass    1 ♦      Pass    1 ♠
        1 N.T.  2 ♣      Pass    4 ♠
        Pass    Pass     Pass
            Opening lead—♦ A
```

Hand No. 105

West's one no-trump was the unusual no-trump, designed to show length in the unbid suits. It could not be a real no-trump, since he had passed to start.

Jack Howell of Toronto, sitting South, jumped to four spades after his partner had opened the bidding in diamonds and gone to two clubs over Jack's one spade. Jack's jump was a slight over-bid but most of the other South players in the World Championship trials reached the same contract. The difference was that most of the others went down two, while Jack actually made it.

West opened the diamond ace and continued with the king. The lead showed a diamond doubleton, because he would have led the king first if he had had more than two. With two tricks tucked away, West led the eight of hearts.

East played the king and Jack dropped the queen. There was no reason for this false-card to work, but the play of the nine of hearts would have been no better.

However, when East saw the queen dropped, he panicked or had one of those brainstorms that seems to afflict even the best players. Instead of cashing his ace of hearts, he led a low diamond.

Now Jack reviewed the bidding and decided that West would hold five cards each in clubs and hearts for his unusual no-trump bid. And he had noted West's lead of the ace-king of the suit. There was no doubt that West had no more diamonds.

Jack ruffed with the eight of trumps. That held, showing that the ten of trumps was in the East hand. Jack led a spade to dummy's ace and ruffed a diamond to return to his hand. This time he used the nine of trumps.

He drew trumps and claimed the balance.

The defense, of course, can get into the false-card act, as shown in Hand No. 106. This was made in the 1964 International play.

North and South had slightly overbid, but the unsound slam would have made, had South known the distribution and used the right line of play.

South captured the opening heart in dummy. He ruffed a

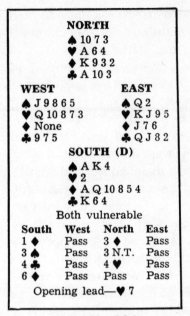

NORTH
♠ 10 7 3
♥ A 6 4
♦ K 9 3 2
♣ A 10 3

WEST
♠ J 9 8 6 5
♥ Q 10 8 7 3
♦ None
♣ 9 7 5

EAST
♠ Q 2
♥ K J 9 5
♦ J 7 6
♣ Q J 8 2

SOUTH (D)
♠ A K 4
♥ 2
♦ A Q 10 8 5 4
♣ K 6 4

Both vulnerable

South	West	North	East
1 ♦	Pass	3 ♦	Pass
3 ♠	Pass	3 N.T.	Pass
4 ♣	Pass	4 ♥	Pass
6 ♦	Pass	Pass	Pass

Opening lead—♥ 7

Hand No. 106

second heart in his hand, drew trumps with three leads, noting that West discarded a spade and two hearts. Then he ruffed dummy's last heart.

His correct line of play would have been to cash the top spades and clubs and lead a third club. East would have had to win with only the thirteenth heart and the thirteenth club to lead. Either would give South a ruff in one hand and the discard of the losing spade in the other.

But East was aware of this danger, and when South played his ace of spades, East dropped his queen.

This put the hand under a different light. South decided that the queen was a singleton. So, instead of leading out his king of spades, he played the king of clubs and went to dummy with the ace of that suit and led another club.

East had to take the trick and he set the hand by leading the deuce of spades. South could not get his ruff and discard, and he could not eat the third spade because the jack was in the West hand.

Hand No. 107 shows one of the most sensational false-card "swindles" we have ever seen. It was sent us by Gordon Keel of Vancouver, British Columbia.

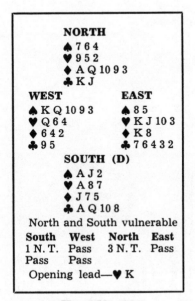

NORTH
♠ 7 6 4
♥ 9 5 2
♦ A Q 10 9 3
♣ K J

WEST
♠ K Q 10 9 3
♥ Q 6 4
♦ 6 4 2
♣ 9 5

EAST
♠ 8 5
♥ K J 10 3
♦ K 8
♣ 7 6 4 3 2

SOUTH (D)
♠ A J 2
♥ A 8 7
♦ J 7 5
♣ A Q 10 8

North and South vulnerable

South	West	North	East
1 N. T.	Pass	3 N. T.	Pass
Pass	Pass		

Opening lead—♥ K

Hand No. 107

West opens the king of spades against South's three no-trump contract. East drops the five and South has apparent alternates. He can win with the ace or duck with the deuce. Neither play looks very good.

If he takes the ace he will have to get around to the diamond finesse. East will win with his king and four spade tricks will doom South to defeat.

If he ducks with the deuce West will surely shift away from spades and undoubtedly will shift to a heart. A heart lead plus heart continuation will give the defense one spade, one diamond and three hearts for the same losing result.

The ace play does look better. If spades are 6-1 East won't have a spade to return; if the spades are 4-3 the defense can only collect three spade tricks.

The use of the word "alternates" implies only two choices, but

South holds three spades. Suppose he plays the jack? Sheer idiocy? If so, it is the sort of idiocy that is really genius.

West will certainly lead a second spade. He will read his partner's five-spot as second highest of three and declarer's jack as from ace-jack doubleton.

South will take his ace, lose his diamond finesse and collect enough tricks for four no-trump irrespective of what East returns.

In the 1964 Fort Worth, Texas, regional tournament practically every South player wound up at four spades after a club opening by East, as shown in Hand No. 108.

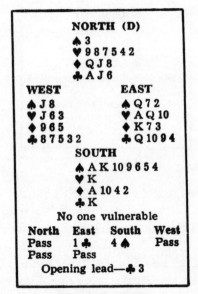

NORTH (D)
♠ 3
♥ 9 8 7 5 4 2
♦ Q J 8
♣ A J 6

WEST
♠ J 8
♥ J 6 3
♦ 9 6 5
♣ 8 7 5 3 2

EAST
♠ Q 7 2
♥ A Q 10
♦ K 7 3
♣ Q 10 9 4

SOUTH
♠ A K 10 9 6 5 4
♥ K
♦ A 10 4 2
♣ K

No one vulnerable

North	East	South	West
Pass	1 ♣	4 ♠	Pass
Pass	Pass		

Opening lead—♣ 3

Hand No. 108

After the three of clubs opening, most careless, penny-pinching declarers would play the six from dummy. They would win with the king and lead ace, king and another spade. East would be in with the queen and, for want of anything better to do, would lead out his ace of hearts. This would drop South's king, and East would lead another heart. South would have to play diamonds from his own hand and wind up making his contract right on the nose.

Alert declarers would call for the ace of clubs from dummy at trick one. This would sacrifice their king but let them in dummy to lead a diamond. They would pick up the king of diamonds this way and make a valuable extra trick.

Malcolm Brachman of Dallas succeeded in making six by playing dummy's jack of clubs. East covered with the queen. Malcolm won with the king as he had to, but he had planted the idea firmly in East's brain that the king of clubs could not be a singleton. Hence, when East got in with the queen of trumps, he led his ten of clubs to knock out dummy's ace. This gave Malcolm a chance to discard his king of hearts and also finesse diamonds to make two overtricks and a top score. It was a neat swindle.

Malcolm's play should not have succeeded. Note that West had opened the three of clubs. Assuming that West discarded the deuce of clubs on the third spade, East should mark his partner with five clubs. But Malcolm had relied on the diversion created by his jack play.

It does not pay to waste high cards, but it pays even less to hang on to one that is useless, as shown in Hand No. 109.

West opened the king of diamonds against South's four-spade contract and continued with the ace, after East played the deuce and South the five. A third diamond lead allowed South to discard a club. West, unfortunately, held both the ace and the queen of clubs so that South's last two tricks were both losers. A player can't lose four tricks and make a four-spade contract.

Had South been alert, he would have realized that the queen of diamonds was a worthless asset and dropped it on West's king.

West might have continued diamonds in any event, and South's false-card would have made no difference. On the other hand, West might have fallen for it. Then West would have shifted to a heart or to a trump. This would have given South a chance to discard his second diamond on dummy's third heart.

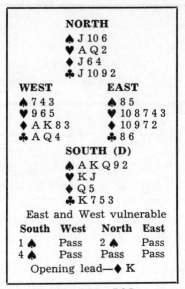

NORTH
♠ J 10 6
♥ A Q 2
♦ J 6 4
♣ J 10 9 2

WEST
♠ 7 4 3
♥ 9 6 5
♦ A K 8 3
♣ A Q 4

EAST
♠ 8 5
♥ 10 8 7 4 3
♦ 10 9 7 2
♣ 8 6

SOUTH (D)
♠ A K Q 9 2
♥ K J
♦ Q 5
♣ K 7 5 3

East and West vulnerable

South	West	North	East
1 ♠	Pass	2 ♠	Pass
4 ♠	Pass	Pass	Pass

Opening lead—♦ K

Hand No. 109

South still would have to lose two club tricks, but a player can lose three tricks and make a four-spade contract.

When someone is called a "book" player, the term means that he knows the basic rules and follows them blindly. A book player will do better in the long run than a man who plays catch-as-catch-can bridge, but he will never be a really great player until he knows when to throw away the book and follow his own best judgment.

Look at Hand No. 110 and imagine yourself in the West seat.

Your opponents have reached five clubs after your partner made an opening bid of one spade and you gave him a minimum raise. What do you lead?

The book player will open the three of spades because the books say to open the fourth best of your partner's suit unless you hold either the ace or touching honors — the king-queen, queen-jack or jack-ten. As a rule this is a good lead, but in this

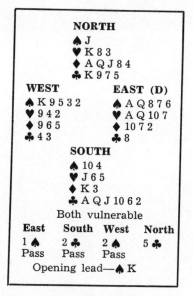

NORTH
♠ J
♥ K 8 3
♦ A Q J 8 4
♣ K 9 7 5

WEST
♠ K 9 5 3 2
♥ 9 4 2
♦ 9 6 5
♣ 4 3

EAST (D)
♠ A Q 8 7 6
♥ A Q 10 7
♦ 10 7 2
♣ 8

SOUTH
♠ 10 4
♥ J 6 5
♦ K 3
♣ A Q J 10 6 2

Both vulnerable

East	South	West	North
1 ♠	2 ♣	2 ♠	5 ♣
Pass	Pass	Pass	

Opening lead—♠ K

Hand No. 110

case the book player will watch South chalk up game and rubber.

East will win the first trick and your side will not take any further tricks unless he cashes his ace of hearts immediately. With an ace-queen tenace over the king of hearts in dummy, East is unlikely to lead out his ace.

If West is a reasoning player he will realize that this is no time for book leads. He will open his king of spades, hoping to hold the trick and find out which red suit to shift to.

And West will set the hand because he will see that the proper shift is to hearts and that his partner will take two more tricks if he holds the ace-queen.

14

Duplicate and Match Points

ONE of the basic principles of match-point play is that you compete for match points, not actual points, and that you get one match point for each player you beat on a particular hand, not for how much you beat him by. One overtrick in a part-score contract may compensate for a lost slam. In rubber bridge it won't. Thirty-point losses mean little. Large losses mean everything.

Hand No. 111 would be played differently in rubber bridge and in tournament play.

A rubber-bridge player would win the heart opening in dummy and draw trumps. Then he would lead a club from his hand and play dummy's ten. Assuming that East won the trick and returned a heart, the rubber-bridge player would win and lead to dummy's ace of clubs, hoping to drop the other missing honor in the suit. If this failed he would concede a heart and a diamond and chalk up game and rubber.

A match-point player would also lead his last club, but would finesse dummy's jack. If it lost and East returned a heart, declarer South would have thrown away a trick worth 720 points, but if it worked he would have gained only 30 points.

Why should he take this risk? Because he would have seen that every pair in the room would be in four spades and that the match-point gain involved in the play would be the same as the

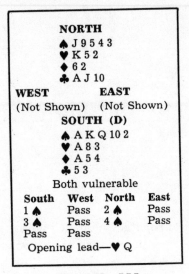

Hand No. 111

match-point loss. But the finesse for the second club honor would be twice as likely to succeed as to fail. Even if it failed, East might not have a heart to lead back to his partner.

At rubber bridge, in a bad contract, you try to make it even though you may go down several extra tricks if things don't go as expected. In duplicate, there are occasions when you should accept a small penalty with good grace because you can expect a good match-point score.

In Hand No. 112, South's three no-trump is a reasonable contract and he has every right to assume that most other South players will be there.

West opens the seven of spades. East takes his ace and returns the nine. West wins with the king and leads back the ten to clear the suit.

South is certain, from the fact that East returned the nine, that West started with five spades and that West's play of the king showed that he held a sure entry for the last two spades.

Thus, South knows that if he knocks out the ace of clubs he

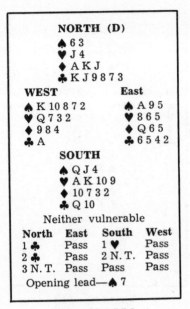

NORTH (D)
♠ 6 3
♥ J 4
♦ A K J
♣ K J 9 8 7 3

WEST
♠ K 10 8 7 2
♥ Q 7 3 2
♦ 9 8 4
♣ A

East
♠ A 9 5
♥ 8 6 5
♦ Q 6 5
♣ 6 5 4 2

SOUTH
♠ Q J 4
♥ A K 10 9
♦ 10 7 3 2
♣ Q 10

Neither vulnerable

North	East	South	West
1 ♣	Pass	1 ♥	Pass
2 ♣	Pass	2 N. T.	Pass
3 N. T.	Pass	Pass	Pass

Opening lead—♠ 7

Hand No. 112

will be down one trick. He also notes that if everything goes
well, he can play diamonds and hearts and make his contract
without using his clubs. Two successful finesses and a satisfactory
diamond break are needed.

In rubber bridge, South should try. He has one chance in
four or five for success and he risks only a few extra fifty-point
tricks.

In duplicate, he should settle for down one and beat those
who tried to make their contracts and went down more.

All is not roses for expert duplicate players. In Hand No. 113
most experts will go down two tricks at a cinch three no-trump
contract in a vain effort to pick up one thirty-point overtrick.

In either rubber bridge or duplicate South will win the opening spade lead in his own hand and go after the club suit. A
rubber-bridge player will be careful to overtake his queen of
clubs (after first playing the king) with dummy's ace. This play

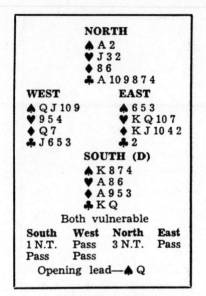

NORTH
♠ A 2
♥ J 3 2
♦ 8 6
♣ A 10 9 8 7 4

WEST
♠ Q J 10 9
♥ 9 5 4
♦ Q 7
♣ J 6 5 3

EAST
♠ 6 5 3
♥ K Q 10 7
♦ K J 10 4 2
♣ 2

SOUTH (D)
♠ K 8 7 4
♥ A 8 6
♦ A 9 5 3
♣ K Q

Both vulnerable

South	West	North	East
1 N.T.	Pass	3 N.T.	Pass
Pass	Pass		

Opening lead—♠ Q

Hand No. 113

will cost him a trick if the clubs break 3-2 but will guarantee five club tricks if they break 4-1. Five clubs plus two spades plus two red aces makes a total of nine, which is all a rubber-bridge player will need for game and rubber. He will leave the extra thirty points for a sixth club trick to the sweepers.

An expert duplicate player will reason differently. He will note that he has a very normal no-trump opening and that his partner has an automatic raise to three no-trump. He will reason that a queen of spades opening lead is pretty standard and that every other South player in the room will also be playing three no-trump against a spade lead.

The chance of a 4-1 break is less than thirty percent and South will play for the overtrick. He will be wrong this time but right most of the time.

Hand No. 114 is another one that shows the difference between rubber bridge and duplicate.

The East and West hands are not shown because they don't

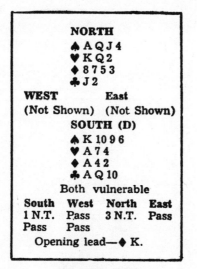

NORTH
♠ A Q J 4
♥ K Q 2
♦ 8 7 5 3
♣ J 2

WEST   East
(Not Shown) (Not Shown)

SOUTH (D)
♠ K 10 9 6
♥ A 7 4
♦ A 4 2
♣ A Q 10

Both vulnerable

South	West	North	East
1 N.T.	Pass	3 N.T.	Pass
Pass	Pass		

Opening lead—♦ K.

Hand No. 114

affect the correct play — merely the final result.

West opens the king of diamonds and continues with the queen after South ducks. East discards a heart and South takes his ace. He cashes the hearts and spades, winding up in dummy, and watches West's discards carefully while doing this.

Everyone will be down to four cards at this point. A rubber-bridge player will throw West in with a diamond in order to force a club lead up to his ace-queen, assuming that he can do so with safety. But if West has come down to three diamonds and a club, the rubber-bridge player will play to his ace of clubs in hope that West's singleton club is the king. In any event the rubber-bridge player is not going to jeopardize his game for possible overtricks.

The duplicate player will note that, assuming spades broke 3-2, all declarers at four spades could lose the club finesse and make four odd or win the club finesse and make five, thus taking the club finesse with safety.

He will come down to the same end situation; if he sees that West is hanging on to two clubs, he will throw him in for the end play on the assumption that one of those two clubs is the king. But if West comes down to three diamonds and one club the chances are that South will risk his whole contract in an effort to make five no-trump.

Why will he do this? Because he is sure that most North-South pairs will be in four spades, not three no-trump, and that three no-trump made on the nose will be just as bad a score as three no-trump down one.

Hand No. 115 represents a good slam, but only one pair in the international team trials in 1965 reached this contract, and they got there for a most unusual reason.

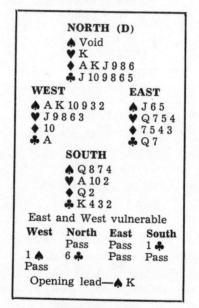

NORTH (D)
♠ Void
♥ K
♦ A K J 9 8 6
♣ J 10 9 8 6 5

WEST
♠ A K 10 9 3 2
♥ J 9 8 6 3
♦ 10
♣ A

EAST
♠ J 6 5
♥ Q 7 5 4
♦ 7 5 4 3
♣ Q 7

SOUTH
♠ Q 8 7 4
♥ A 10 2
♦ Q 2
♣ K 4 3 2

East and West vulnerable

West	North	East	South
	Pass	Pass	1 ♣
1 ♠	6 ♣	Pass	Pass
Pass			

Opening lead—♠ K

Hand No. 115

Eight of the nine Norths opened with one diamond and their partners responded one spade. Then the bidding would proceed to five clubs, irrespective of whether or not West got into the competition. North would like the distribution, but be nervous about his lack of high cards and the fact that his partner's first bid had been in spades.

Arthur Robinson of Philadelphia, sitting North, did not open with one diamond. He passed. His partner, Bobby Jordan, opened with one club. West overcalled with one spade and Arthur decided there was no scientific way to bid the hand and jumped to six clubs.

Bobby ruffed the opening spade in dummy, led the jack of clubs and let it ride. West took his singleton ace and led a heart, whereupon Bobby spread his hand and claimed the rest of the tricks.

Bobby had better than a fifty percent chance on the hand because his play would make the slam any time East held the queen of trumps. It would also have worked if East had held the singleton ace of trumps.

Going back to the trials a year earlier, we find a hand that shows the pitfalls of duplicate. The hand, No. 116, had two types of bidding. Four South players chose to overcall East's one-heart opening with two clubs, four West players chose to double and four South players had no place to go but down.

The normal defense started with a heart opening. East would win with the king and continue by cashing first his ace, then his king of spades to show that he had no other spades.

Next, East would play the ace of hearts and a small heart for West to ruff. West would play a third spade for East to ruff. This gave the defense the first six tricks and they would still collect one diamond and one trump for an 800-point profit.

Five South players were wise enough to keep their mouths shut on this hand. In all cases, East wound up at a two-diamond contract and made either four or five.

Ozzie Jacoby was one of the South players who did not over-call. It has long been a principle of his that it does not pay to overcall at the two level unless he has a good six-card suit or better. Those who do so are playing with loaded dice because their opponents can easily outbid with a higher suit, unless they choose to double.

The five players who failed to overcall were rewarded by a

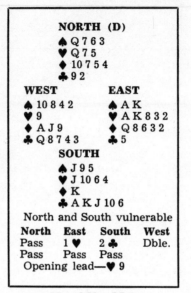

NORTH (D)
♠ Q 7 6 3
♥ Q 7 5
♦ 10 7 5 4
♣ 9 2

WEST
♠ 10 8 4 2
♥ 9
♦ A J 9
♣ Q 8 7 4 3

EAST
♠ A K
♥ A K 8 3 2
♦ Q 8 6 3 2
♣ 5

SOUTH
♠ J 9 5
♥ J 10 6 4
♦ K
♣ A K J 10 6

North and South vulnerable

North	East	South	West
Pass	1 ♥	2 ♣	Dble.
Pass	Pass	Pass	

Opening lead—♥ 9

Hand No. 116

gain of six International Match Points each. Their unfortunate opponents were charged with six IMPs each through no fault of their own. There was nothing they could do against silent opponents.

Furthermore, while three of the East-West pairs made five diamonds, the game was not the sort that anyone in his right mind would want to bid. Three no-trump would also make, but there was no way to bid it unless all the cards were in sight.

Hand No. 117 is also from the same trials and again it shows how luck plays a big part even in a game where skill is reckoned to be the deciding factor.

Most South players chose to pass on this hand, but one of them opened with a heart. And after he was started, South found it impossible to stop as North continued to make one forcing bid after another.

Eventually South found himself at six hearts, a contract that looked very uncomfortable.

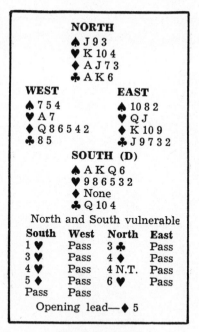

NORTH
♠ J 9 3
♥ K 10 4
♦ A J 7 3
♣ A K 6

WEST
♠ 7 5 4
♥ A 7
♦ Q 8 6 5 4 2
♣ 8 5

EAST
♠ 10 8 2
♥ Q J
♦ K 10 9
♣ J 9 7 3 2

SOUTH (D)
♠ A K Q 6
♥ 9 8 6 5 3 2
♦ None
♣ Q 10 4

North and South vulnerable

South	West	North	East
1 ♥	Pass	3 ♣	Pass
3 ♥	Pass	4 ♦	Pass
4 ♥	Pass	4 N.T.	Pass
5 ♦	Pass	6 ♥	Pass
Pass	Pass		

Opening lead—♦ 5

Hand No. 117

He ruffed the opening diamond and led a heart toward dummy. West played low and South rose with dummy's king. East played his jack and the second trump lead bumped the ace and queen in one fell swoop. After that South claimed the rest of the tricks and his contract.

One other North-South pair managed to reach the same horrible slam and each slam bidder was rewarded with twelve IMPS, while their opponents were penalized the same amount.

On the same hand, one East player found himself playing a five-diamond contract. He got there after his partner doubled a four-diamond call by South and North had redoubled.

South cashed three spade tricks and shifted to a heart, won by North's king. A second heart put East in dummy. He led a low trump and finessed his ten. Then he played a club, whereupon the defense cashed two club tricks and led a third club for dummy to ruff.

Another low trump was led from dummy and North made the correct play of the ace. At this point North's correct play was to lead a low trump. East would win in his own hand and North would make his jack of trumps. But even experts go wrong. North led his last heart and East made the rest of the tricks but was still down five tricks or 900 points in the score.

When your opponent gets into an unbeatable contract, as in Hand No. 118, good defense must try to keep him from making an overtrick. In rubber bridge an overtrick represents a mere thirty points as a rule, but in duplicate it may mean the difference between a good score and a bad one.

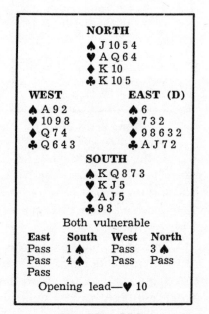

NORTH
♠ J 10 5 4
♥ A Q 6 4
♦ K 10
♣ K 10 5

WEST
♠ A 9 2
♥ 10 9 8
♦ Q 7 4
♣ Q 6 4 3

EAST (D)
♠ 6
♥ 7 3 2
♦ 9 8 6 3 2
♣ A J 7 2

SOUTH
♠ K Q 8 7 3
♥ K J 5
♦ A J 5
♣ 9 8

Both vulnerable

East	South	West	North
Pass	1 ♠	Pass	3 ♠
Pass	4 ♠	Pass	Pass
Pass			

Opening lead—♥ 10

Hand No. 118

The Jacobys were partners when this hand was played, with Jim sitting West and Ozzie sitting East.

Jim opened the ten of hearts and South could see when dummy went down that he could not misplay the hand. South called for the ace from dummy and Ozzie dropped the deuce.

The four of spades was led from dummy and Jim let South's
king hold, hoping to give Ozzie a chance to signal whether to
lead clubs or diamonds on the next trump lead. Out came the
second spade and Jim played his ace.

Ozzie had to signal but it was not easy. If he dropped the
seven of clubs, Jim might mistake it for the lowest club in his
hand. There was a better way to signal. Ozzie dropped the
deuce of diamonds, which gave Jim the information he needed.
Ozzie had dropped two discouraging deuces, and therefore he
did not want leads in hearts or diamonds. Perhaps Ozzie did not
want a club lead either, but at least that lead was indicated. Out
came a club and Ozzie cashed two club tricks to hold declarer
to his contract.

A diamond or a heart lead would have permitted declarer to
pull Jim's last trump and discard a club on dummy's fourth
heart, giving him an overtrick.

Hand No. 119 was Board 36 of the International match between Italy and America in 1965, and it shows that tournament
play is not always the same even between two groups of experts.

Both the Italian and the American Souths opened with one
spade, in spite of the fact that they held only ten high-card
points and the final contract in each case was three spades. Although that contract is not the safest in the world, it can be
made because of the favorable location of the king of clubs
and the queen of hearts. Curiously enough, Italy made four,
while the American player went down one.

The American West opened the deuce of trumps against the
Italian South, who won the trick in his hand and led the deuce
of clubs. West took his ace and cashed two diamonds and led a
second trump, whereupon the Italian declarer was able to set
up dummy's long clubs for three heart discards.

Now let's see what happened to the American South. We
don't think he played badly.

Avarelli of Italy opened the jack of clubs against the three-
spade contract. It never occurred to South that Avarelli would

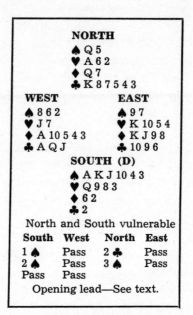

Hand No. 119

have led away from the ace of clubs, so South played low in hope that East would have to play the ace on the first or second club lead (assuming that East had it, of course).

On the second trick West shifted to the deuce of spades. Declarer won with the jack, entered dummy with the queen, ruffed a club, drew trumps and went after hearts. The queen of hearts was in a satisfactory position, behind the king, but South still had to lose two heart tricks and two diamonds and was down one.

15

Unusual Plays and Hands

WE have spread quite a number of unusual hands and unusual plays through this book because they fit well as illustrations in particular categories. But some hands do not fall into any category and the plays themselves are almost classics.

The late Ely Culbertson was not only one of the greatest bridge theorists and writers of all time, but he was one of the most imaginative players. His motto at the card table might well have been "Always Attack." At least he had profound faith in the idea that you will never get anywhere if you do not take chances.

Hand No. 120 is one that helped his team win the national board-a-match team championship of 1931.

Ely sat West and opened with a one-spade bid. He had a sound opening bid in the Culbertson, or any other, system, and he was rather astonished to find his opponents at three no-trump when it came his turn to bid again.

He saw there was no point in taking further action because his partner gave no sign of holding much. He passed.

His normal lead would be a spade, but Ely felt that South would not have jumped to three no-trump with only one spade stopper. If Ely had led a spade no one could possibly criticize him, but Ely thrived on criticism and furthermore he wanted to win.

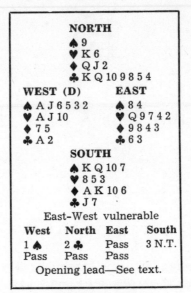

NORTH
♠ 9
♥ K 6
♦ Q J 2
♣ K Q 10 9 8 5 4

WEST (D)
♠ A J 6 5 3 2
♥ A J 10
♦ 7 5
♣ A 2

EAST
♠ 8 4
♥ Q 9 7 4 2
♦ 9 8 4 3
♣ 6 3

SOUTH
♠ K Q 10 7
♥ 8 5 3
♦ A K 10 6
♣ J 7

East–West vulnerable

West	North	East	South
1 ♠	2 ♣	Pass	3 N.T.
Pass	Pass	Pass	

Opening lead—See text.

Hand No. 120

He led the jack of hearts.

South gave the hand the old college try and went up with dummy's king, but nothing could rescue him. South had to break the clubs and Ely took his ace and continued hearts so that his side eventually collected six tricks for down two against South.

Ely's team partners, Johnny Rau and Billy Barrett, also reached three no-trump with the North-South cards but they had a different player for the opening lead. Their West opponent opened a spade and Johnny, who sat South, made five no-trump when West failed to take his ace of hearts.

Hand No. 121 is one of the luckiest grand slams in history, and this may be an understatement. It was North's fault. His bidding may look strange but it was because he was slightly hard of hearing.

When East opened the bidding with one heart, North thought he had said "Pass," and therefore bid on the assumption that

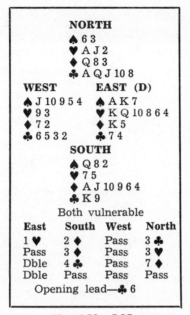

NORTH
♠ 6 3
♥ A J 2
♦ Q 8 3
♣ A Q J 10 8

WEST
♠ J 10 9 5 4
♥ 9 3
♦ 7 2
♣ 6 5 3 2

EAST (D)
♠ A K 7
♥ K Q 10 8 6 4
♦ K 5
♣ 7 4

SOUTH
♠ Q 8 2
♥ 7 5
♦ A J 10 9 6 4
♣ K 9

Both vulnerable

East	South	West	North
1 ♥	2 ♦	Pass	3 ♣
Pass	3 ♦	Pass	3 ♥
Dble	4 ♣	Pass	7 ♦
Dble	Pass	Pass	Pass

Opening lead—♣ 6

Hand No. 121

Walter Malowan, who sat South, had opened with a forcing two-diamond bid.

East caught on and his double was an attempt to punish Walter, but it was a great mistake. West thought the double called for a club lead.

West led a club, whereupon Walter was able to make the grand slam. All it required was a diamond finesse, a 2-2 trump break, a favorable opening lead and the ace-king of spades and king-queen of hearts in the East hand so that a squeeze could be developed.

Walter won the club lead in dummy and led the queen of diamonds. East covered and a second lead exhausted the adverse trumps.

Walter next ran off the rest of the club suit while discarding two low spades and a low heart from his own hand. Then came the rest of the trumps. The discards from dummy were two spades and a heart so that dummy was left with the ace-jack of hearts and East wished he was playing some other game.

East could not protect both major suits and Walter made the slam. Had East not doubled, West undoubtedly would have led a heart, which was East's opening bid, and the squeeze could not have taken place.

After a discussion of four-card suit openings in our newspaper column, a reader from Maine wrote:

"I just hate to bid four-card suits. It seems that my partner always raises me and I find myself playing, unsuccessfully, with four trumps opposite three."

Ozzie's answer was that people who get in such fixes should learn to live with them. Even a 4-2 fit works out once in a few hundred times.

As an example, Hand No. 122, illustrates a hand Ozzie played for a Navy team against a combined Army and civilian team when he was on duty in Japan during the Korean War. His partner outranked him in the Navy, but was determined to play as few dummies as possible.

```
                 NORTH (D)
                 ♠ K J
                 ♥ 4 3
                 ♦ A K J 4 3
                 ♣ 9 6 5 2
      WEST                    EAST
      ♠ 8 6 5                 ♠ 7 4 3 2
      ♥ A K 9 6               ♥ Q 10 8 5 2
      ♦ 10 7 5                ♦ 9 8
      ♣ J 10 3                ♣ K Q
                 SOUTH
                 ♠ A Q 10 9
                 ♥ J 7
                 ♦ Q 6 2
                 ♣ A 8 7 4
              Both vulnerable
```

North	East	South	West
1 ♦	Pass	1 ♠	Pass
2 ♠	Pass	4 ♠	Pass
Pass	Pass		

Opening lead—♥ K

Hand No. 122

Hence, Commander Jacoby found himself playing four spades with four trumps opposite two. But it was the only game contract that could make and was arrived at because North wanted to be dummy.*

West cashed two hearts and continued the suit. Ozzie ruffed in dummy and discarded a club from his hand. Then he drew trumps and discarded his other two losers on the long diamonds.

At the other table North and South gambled on three no-trump and the Navy pair cashed five heart tricks before surrendering the lead.

Hand No. 123 goes back some thirty years to the days before Blackwood. The hero is the late Sherman Stearns of New York, winner of several national titles in the thirties and one of the greatest players of all time.

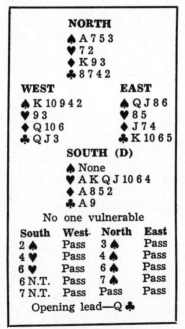

NORTH
♠ A 7 5 3
♥ 7 2
♦ K 9 3
♣ 8 7 4 2

WEST	EAST
♠ K 10 9 4 2	♠ Q J 8 6
♥ 9 3	♥ 8 5
♦ Q 10 6	♦ J 7 4
♣ Q J 3	♣ K 10 6 5

SOUTH (D)
♠ None
♥ A K Q J 10 6 4
♦ A 8 5 2
♣ A 9

No one vulnerable

South	West	North	East
2 ♠	Pass	3 ♠	Pass
4 ♥	Pass	4 ♠	Pass
6 ♥	Pass	6 ♠	Pass
6 N.T.	Pass	7 ♠	Pass
7 N.T.	Pass	Pass	Pass

Opening lead—Q ♣

Hand No. 123

* Note by Jim Jacoby: "It is never hard to get to be dummy when you are Dad's partner. I don't know anyone who likes to play hands better than he."

The game was rubber bridge and as Sherman picked up his hand in the South seat he said to himself, "I have no spades." But the words "Two spades" came out of his mouth.

When his partner raised him, he tried to correct his mistake by bidding four hearts, six hearts and six no-trump, and eventually found himself at seven no-trump when his partner persisted on bidding spades. North had to give up at seven no-trump.

The contract was apparently hopeless. Sherman could count eleven tricks in top cards and a possible twelfth, if diamonds broke.

It seems that Sherman never gave away the fact that something was wrong with the bidding, and as he ran off heart tricks each opponent threw away a diamond in order to hang on to spades.

The rest was simply a matter of pulling them in.

Of course East and West should have known there was something peculiar about the two-spade opening because he showed up with seven hearts and the ace of clubs, but neither was able to visualize the spade void.

Hand No. 124 was played by Mr. and Mrs. Oswald Jacoby before Jim was born. Ozzie, who sat South, describes the hand in his own words:

"Mrs. Jacoby was just learning contract, hence my two no-trump response to her opening diamond. It was and still is her custom never to take me out of no-trump contracts, but I had explained there were exceptions to all rules. This time she ran to four diamonds when I was doubled at three no-trump.

"She would have made four diamonds, had I let her stay there, but I tried four hearts. She had bid hearts in response to my two no-trump. Then after West gave my bid the treatment, I finally showed my club suit at the five level.

"Mrs. Jacoby went back to diamonds and I went to six clubs, whereupon she decided to let me work out my own problems.

"But it didn't turn out to be much of a problem. I played a low diamond from dummy on the first trick and ruffed in my

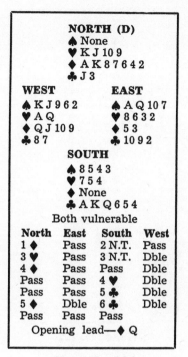

NORTH (D)
♠ None
♥ K J 10 9
♦ A K 8 7 6 4 2
♣ J 3

WEST
♠ K J 9 6 2
♥ A Q
♦ Q J 10 9
♣ 8 7

EAST
♠ A Q 10 7
♥ 8 6 3 2
♦ 5 3
♣ 10 9 2

SOUTH
♠ 8 5 4 3
♥ 7 5 4
♦ None
♣ A K Q 6 5 4

Both vulnerable

North	East	South	West
1 ♦	Pass	2 N.T.	Pass
3 ♥	Pass	3 N.T.	Dble
4 ♦	Pass	Pass	Dble
Pass	Pass	4 ♥	Dble
Pass	Pass	5 ♣	Dble
5 ♦	Dble	6 ♣	Dble
Pass	Pass	Pass	

Opening lead—♦ Q

Hand No. 124

own hand. Then I led a heart. West played the queen and I was in dummy with the king. A ruff of a second low diamond cleared up that suit and I led a second heart to West's ace.

"Eventually I pulled trumps and made my brilliantly bid slam."

Harold S. (Mike) Vanderbilt invented the game of contract bridge in 1927. Ozzie played with him at Newport recently and reports that at the age of eighty-one he still handles the dummy as well as anyone.

Ozzie says that Mike has speeded up his play because although he could play for hours on end in the old days, he can only play short sessions today.

Ozzie played the Vanderbilt club with Mike out of deference to his partner, and the bidding of Hand No. 125 is based on that convention.

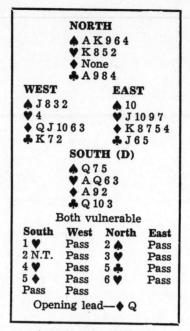

NORTH
♠ A K 9 6 4
♥ K 8 5 2
♦ None
♣ A 9 8 4

WEST
♠ J 8 3 2
♥ 4
♦ Q J 10 6 3
♣ K 7 2

EAST
♠ 10
♥ J 10 9 7
♦ K 8 7 5 4
♣ J 6 5

SOUTH (D)
♠ Q 7 5
♥ A Q 6 3
♦ A 9 2
♣ Q 10 3

Both vulnerable

South	West	North	East
1 ♥	Pass	2 ♠	Pass
2 N.T.	Pass	3 ♥	Pass
4 ♥	Pass	5 ♣	Pass
5 ♦	Pass	6 ♥	Pass
Pass	Pass		

Opening lead—♦ Q

Hand No. 125

The six-heart contract was a good one; even seven would have been made with good breaks, but as you can see the good breaks were conspicuous by their absence. Nevertheless, Mike managed to bring the slam home.

He ruffed the opening diamond in dummy and played king and another heart. West showed out, but this didn't faze Mike. He ruffed his last low diamond, led out dummy's king of spades and continued with a spade toward his own hand.

At this point East made his best play. He ruffed in. Had East failed to ruff there would have been no further problems.

Mike was careful to drop his queen of spades in order to un-block for an eventual finesse against West's jack. Now East made his last try. He led the five of clubs. If Mike had played the queen it would have been curtains, but Mike put in the ten. After that play the slam was a cinch.

Often the manner in which a player brings home a contract

looks "lucky," but as we have pointed out there are usually several lines of play open to a declarer. Skill in selecting the right one will often bring home a dubious contract. Hand No. 125 is a case in point.

The question marks in Hand No. 126 are not typographical errors. South made the contract without finding out who had what in clubs.

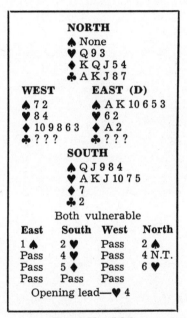

NORTH
♠ None
♥ Q 9 3
♦ K Q J 5 4
♣ A K J 8 7

WEST
♠ 7 2
♥ 8 4
♦ 10 9 8 6 3
♣ ? ? ?

EAST (D)
♠ A K 10 6 5 3
♥ 6 2
♦ A 2
♣ ? ? ?

SOUTH
♠ Q J 9 8 4
♥ A K J 10 7 5
♦ 7
♣ 2

Both vulnerable

East	South	West	North
1 ♠	2 ♥	Pass	2 ♠
Pass	4 ♥	Pass	4 N.T.
Pass	5 ♦	Pass	6 ♥
Pass	Pass	Pass	

Opening lead—♥ 4

Hand No. 126

North drove to the slam after South had made a two-heart overcall of East's opening spade bid, and West opened a trump rather than a spade.

South looked over the hand and counted eleven easy tricks, including six trumps, two diamonds, two clubs and a ruff of a spade. He would have counted two ruffs if a trump had not been opened, but defenders do not always cooperate.

South expected a second trump lead after he lost a trick to the ace of diamonds. This did not worry him because he knew that East would hold the ace of diamonds and the ace-king of spades, and he believed that if either opponent held five diamonds it would be West.

His play was a diamond at trick two. East took dummy's jack with his ace and led a second trump. South took the trick and made the rest by what the younger experts call an automatic double squeeze.

He ruffed one spade, discarded two spades on the king and queen of diamonds, ruffed a diamond and ran out the rest of his trumps.

The last trump lead forced West down to two clubs (he started with four, although the diagram shows only three question marks). West had to discard clubs in order to hold on to a diamond. South discarded the last diamond from dummy and the pressure was on East. He had to hang on to a high spade and therefore he discarded down to two clubs. This made dummy's last three clubs winners.

Entries to dummy and the lack thereof bring premature age to bridge players, but in Hand No. 127, one hard-working dummy entry performed yeoman service. The hand was sent to us by Augusta Cantor of New York.

"I was playing rubber bridge," she writes, "and was delighted with my hand. I might have opened with two clubs, but in our game no one ever is allowed to play a one-club contract and I started conservatively.

"West's four-spades was quite a shock. I dislike being shut out and went to five clubs. West opened the ace of spades and shifted to a heart. I took the trick.

"Then I played the ace of clubs and got the bad news about four trumps in East's hand. I cashed my ace, king and queen of hearts, hoping that East would show up with four hearts so that I could get a diamond discard on dummy's jack, but hearts were 3-3.

"In spite of the grim outlook there were possibilities in diamonds. I entered dummy with the queen of clubs and led the

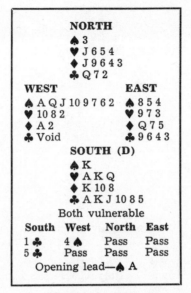

NORTH
- ♠ 3
- ♥ J 6 5 4
- ♦ J 9 6 4 3
- ♣ Q 7 2

WEST
- ♠ A Q J 10 9 7 6 2
- ♥ 10 8 2
- ♦ A 2
- ♣ Void

EAST
- ♠ 8 5 4
- ♥ 9 7 3
- ♦ Q 7 5
- ♣ 9 6 4 3

SOUTH (D)
- ♠ K
- ♥ A K Q
- ♦ K 10 8
- ♣ A K J 10 8 5

Both vulnerable

South	West	North	East
1 ♣	4 ♠	Pass	Pass
5 ♣	Pass	Pass	Pass

Opening lead—♠ A

Hand No. 127

jack of diamonds. East played low and I did likewise. West was in with the ace and he had to give me my contract. A spade lead would give me a ruff and discard and a diamond lead would be up to my king-ten tenace."

Mrs. Cantor's play illustrates that timid players don't win bridge games. The contract was not the best in the world, but far from the worst. One entry in dummy gave double service.

In this hand, West's preemptive overcall forced South to a game contract in clubs. In tournament play overcalls often bring about interesting bidding.

The American Contract Bridge League conducts three nationwide charity games each year. The hands are made up by a computer and played simultaneously all over the continent. Each game is scored locally by match-point scoring.

Hand No. 128 is one of these computer-dealt hands.

Even though both sides were vulnerable, everyone went high in the bidding on this hand. Most North-South players managed

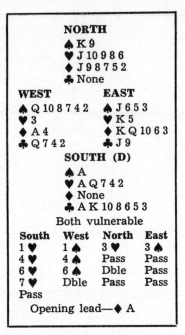

Hand No. 128

to buy the hand at six or seven hearts. Those who bid seven took the heart finesse and made the grand slam. Many who stopped at six refused the finesse and just made their contract.

The best East-West score we heard of resulted from an artificial two-club bid by South, to show a strong hand, but not to show anything about the distribution. West overcalled with two spades and East jumped to four. Because South's two-club bid had been artificial, he had no way to show both his suits and just jumped to six clubs. West passed and South had to lose a club and a heart for down one.

The saddest story of the tournament was that of a West player whose opponent opened with one heart. Apparently that particular player had some prejudice against the club suit and against opening two bids. The bidding proceeded as shown in the diagram until West doubled seven hearts.

South finessed against East's king of hearts and made his grand slam doubled.

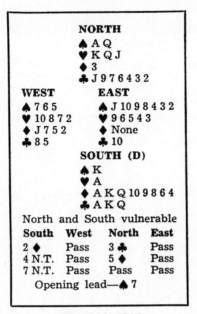

NORTH
♠ A Q
♥ K Q J
♦ 3
♣ J 9 7 6 4 3 2

WEST
♠ 7 6 5
♥ 10 8 7 2
♦ J 7 5 2
♣ 8 5

EAST
♠ J 10 9 8 4 3 2
♥ 9 6 5 4 3
♦ None
♣ 10

SOUTH (D)
♠ K
♥ A
♦ A K Q 10 9 8 6 4
♣ A K Q

North and South vulnerable

South	West	North	East
2 ♦	Pass	3 ♣	Pass
4 N.T.	Pass	5 ♦	Pass
7 N.T.	Pass	Pass	Pass

Opening lead—♠ 7

Hand No. 129

We are indebted to the fertile brain of Bill Root and Larry Rossler for Hand No. 129, which was used in the 1963 intercollegiate tournament.

It was strictly a problem for North and South, who would obtain a bidding par for getting to either seven clubs or seven no-trump. As you can see, seven diamonds won't make because all four missing diamonds are in the West hand.

The play par is obtained if South can see how to make seven no-trump against a directed spade opening.

Of course, South does not have the advantage of seeing the East-West cards, but since it is a contest he can be pretty sure that he can't just spread the hand and claim thirteen tricks.

So he studies the opening lead and decides that someone has stacked all the four enemy diamonds right in back of his own eight. Then how can he make the hand?

He can perform an operation that the late Geoffrey Mott-Smith entitled the "great unblock." He wins the first trick with dummy's ace of spades. Then he discards his ace of hearts on the queen of spades. Then he discards his ace, king and queen of clubs on the king, queen and jack of hearts.

Finally he leads dummy's jack of clubs. It drops East's ten and he runs off clubs up to the last trick, which goes to his own ace of diamonds. The play has risked nothing. If the ten of clubs failed to drop under the jack, he would still have been able to make the grand slam if diamonds would run.

16

How to Pick Up Points

WE have tried in the preceding pages to show that bridge is a lively, competitive, interesting game that develops logic, deduction and imagination. Furthermore, it is fun. Most of the play we have described has merit; some is not recommended.

But have we succeeded in our purpose of showing you how to win? There is one final word of advice that may prove more important than anything else in this respect.

Over the years, we have played with the greatest of experts and the rawest of beginners. We have had more good results from an opponent's attempts to be brilliant than from anything else. Not that brilliancy is out of place at the bridge table, Heaven forbid. But solid, conservative play will dó more for a player in the long run. There are times for sensational plays, even trumping your partner's good ace — which is the subject of many bridge jokes. But most of the time you will find that it pays to play the cards close to your shirt buttons and let the other fellow be excessively cute.

Hand No. 130, in which Jim Jacoby was declarer, illustrates the difference between brilliance and caution.

Jim found himself in an impossible three no-trump contract. That is, it became impossible when a spade was opened and dummy's queen was gobbled up by East's king.

Jim, sitting South, counted six diamond tricks, one spade

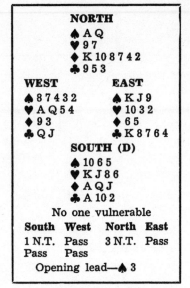

NORTH
♠ A Q
♥ 9 7
♦ K 10 8 7 4 2
♣ 9 5 3

WEST
♠ 8 7 4 3 2
♥ A Q 5 4
♦ 9 3
♣ Q J

EAST
♠ K J 9
♥ 10 3 2
♦ 6 5
♣ K 8 7 6 4

SOUTH (D)
♠ 10 6 5
♥ K J 8 6
♦ A Q J
♣ A 10 2

No one vulnerable

South	West	North	East
1 N.T.	Pass	3 N.T.	Pass
Pass	Pass		

Opening lead—♠ 3

Hand No. 130

trick, one club trick and nothing nearer than the next hand for his ninth trick.

Then East obligingly started to think. Not that this is out of place, because we have endorsed thinking since we learned there was such a thing. But sometimes thinking is based on the wrong premise. Obviously, thought East, partner has a long spade suit and declarer is decidedly weak in this department. Then East came to the conclusion that maybe he should unblock the suit, so that his partner could clobber Jim.

East tossed the pros and cons back and forth and finally lost the argument with himself. He played the jack of spades, setting up Jim's ten for the ninth trick.

Jim was sympathetic, because had he held the queen of hearts and not held the ten of spades, East's unblocking would have set the contract, as East intended it should.

In that case, purely hypothetical, East would have led the jack of spades to knock out dummy's ace, then Jim would have knocked out West's ace of hearts by leading a heart from dummy, forcing the ace with his king-queen-jack of hearts combination. West would take the first trick with the ace, play his ten of spades and East's nine would have dropped. Then two more spade tricks in the West hand would have set Jim.

As the cards actually were dealt, East had nothing to worry about, but he could not see all the cards. He did not know West held the ace and queen of hearts over South's king-jack. Thus, East could have led his nine of spades to knock out the ace of spades in dummy. Jim would have led a heart from dummy, and West would have taken the trick no matter which card of the king-jack combination South played. Then West would have led a small spade and East would play his jack, capturing Jim's ten, and another heart lead would have put West back into the lead to use his two remaining spades.

Thus by playing his jack, East gave South a trick with the ten of spades.

And now, about thinking. When Rattlesnake Pete, the world champion rattlesnake hunter, was asked to tell why he was so good at his profession, he said: "I just try to think like a rattler."

So, if you are going to be a declarer-hunter, or a defender-hunter, it would do well to learn to think like your prey.

In Hand No. 131, look only at the North and West hands. West opens his fourth best in his longest suit, hearts, against South's three no-trump contract.

East plays the queen and South takes the trick with his ace. Then South leads the deuce of diamonds and if West has not learned to think like a bridge player, it will be all over. West will duck and dummy's king will hold the trick. Afterward South will dance home, gathering up five clubs and two spades on the way.

But declarer-hunter West knows how South thinks. He sees that the play is highly unusual and asks himself if South would have taken his line if he had started with the ace-jack-small in hearts. The answer is negative. West knows, of course, that East did not have the jack, because in that case East would have put

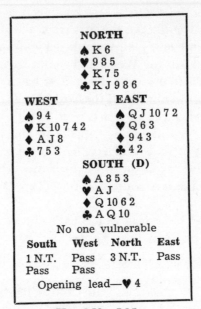

NORTH
♠ K 6
♥ 9 8 5
♦ K 7 5
♣ K J 9 8 6

WEST
♠ 9 4
♥ K 10 7 4 2
♦ A J 8
♣ 7 5 3

EAST
♠ Q J 10 7 2
♥ Q 6 3
♦ 9 4 3
♣ 4 2

SOUTH (D)
♠ A 8 5 3
♥ A J
♦ Q 10 6 2
♣ A Q 10

No one vulnerable

South	West	North	East
1 N.T.	Pass	3 N.T.	Pass
Pass	Pass		

Opening lead—♥ 4

Hand No. 131

the lower of the touching honors on trick one.

West, still thinking like a declarer, now will wonder what South would have done if he had eight tricks and needed a ninth, but had only the ace-jack doubleton of hearts?

West will quickly find the answer. If West were the declarer with the same hand, West would do exactly what South had done.

At this point, declarer-hunter West will rise with his ace of diamonds and lead the king of hearts. South's jack of hearts will be crushed and West will take three more heart tricks.

Don't be brilliant, just think like a bridge player.

Appendix

Evaluation of Hands

The key cards in your hand and your trumps determine how many tricks you are likely to take. Key cards are the ace, king, queen and jack of each suit.

By assigning certain values to each of these cards and to distribution, you can determine fairly closely how strong your hand is. The point count is so simple that even a beginner can learn it and so accurate that an expert cannot afford not to use it.

There are three kinds of points: honor points (high-card points), distribution points, and supporting points.

This table tells you how to count your hand.

High-Card Points

Each ace	4 points
Each king	3 points
Each queen	2 points
Each jack	1 point

Add one point for all four aces.

Distribution Points

Each void (blank suit)	3 points
Each singleton (one card in suit)	2 points
Each doubleton(two in a suit)	1 point

Add one point for each card over four in any suit so strong that you do not need partner's support in establishing it.

Supporting Points

Add one point for each trump over three in responding in support of your partner's suit.

Add one point extra for each singleton or void if you can support your partner's suit.

Liabilities

Do not count distribution points or supporting points in notrump.

In a suit bid, balanced distribution (4-3-3-3) is a liability. Subtracting one point is often a way to offset this liability.

In a hand without aces, or in one where the strength lies entirely in jacks and queens, your point count should be shaved a little. This type of hand is not as strong as the same count in aces and kings.

Key Numbers

Grand slam .... 37 points
Small slam .... 33 points
Minor-suit game (eleven tricks) .... 29 points
Major-suit game (ten tricks) .... 26 points
No-trump game (nine tricks) .... 26 points